SWEETS AND CANDY

Edible

Series Editor: Andrew F. Smith

EDIBLE is a revolutionary series of books dedicated to food and drink that explores the rich history of cuisine. Each book reveals the global history and culture of one type of food or beverage.

Already published

Sweets and Candy

A Global History

Laura Mason

REAKTION BOOKS

For Derek

Published by Reaktion Books Ltd
Unit 32, Waterside
44–48 Wharf Road
London N1 7UX, UK
www.reaktionbooks.co.uk

First published 2018
Copyright © Laura Mason 2018

Printed and bound in China

A catalogue record for this book is available from the British Library

ISBN 978 1 78023 927 9

Contents

I

Sweet, Candy or Confection?

The British know exactly what they mean by a sweet, and North Americans, likewise, are certain about a candy. In their respective cultures each word means a sweet-tasting, interestingly textured, small, sugar-based item. It is eaten with the fingers and does not usually form part of a meal. Dazzling in colour, variable in shape, mostly long-lasting and sometimes tasting very strange, they are much loved by children. These seemingly inconsequential items are freighted with centuries of changing cultural attitudes, social and economic history, emotional attachments and divergent views on the role of sugar in health. Chocolate is an essential part of notions about sweets and candy, but, although extremely popular, it does not form part of this book except in passing. It has its own considerable history and cultural significance, and requires very different skills and equipment to those used with sugar.

'Candy' is a word of ancient derivation that can be traced back over millennia to India. Historians of sugar generally agree that the skill of refining cane juice first developed here, over two thousand years ago, together with a vocabulary of Sanskrit-derived words, including *sakkar* and *khanda*. Both these probably indicated grades of solid sugar with a crystalline

Anon., *Lady Offering Sweetmeats*, 1810–30, oil on calico. An image from Persia, where, together with Egypt and Turkey, wealthy courts were important in developing and transmitting sugarworking skills.

Rock candy on sale in a supermarket in the USA, 2016.

texture. The words were transmitted with the skills of growing and refining sugar westwards through Persia, reaching the Eastern Mediterranean by the tenth century. They eventually gave European languages phrases such as Spanish *azucar cande* and English sugar-candy, describing sugar in a crystalline mass, such as that in sugar loaves. European settlers took sugar to the New World, and 'candy' became the term for small sugary items in North American English.

'Sweet' appears simply to be descriptive of candy: it is sweet to the taste. Some cultures are more interested in the idea than others, notably India, the Middle East and the Anglophone world. But the notion of 'a sweet' is more complex, as one writer found when considering different cultures:

What is a sweet? When I first embarked on my research, it seemed simple. A sweet was a little something you carried around in your pocket to eat outside prescribed mealtimes. But that is a modern, Western idea of a sweet. In fact, every nation has its own idea of what a sweet might be.[1]

As a collective term, 'sweet' is an early nineteenth-century abbreviation of 'sweetmeat' for sweet foods generally. This helps to explain why the word 'sweet' sometimes becomes entangled with dessert, a distinct course in a large meal in Europe, America and areas influenced by European food habits. This non-essential but enjoyable collection of foods took its name from the French *desservir*, originally describing a late medieval habit of leaving servants to clear the table while diners repaired elsewhere for a *digestif* of spiced wine, wafers and sugar-coated spices.

From this simple beginning, Renaissance Italians evolved the *collazione*. This was a lavish, expensive assemblage of sweetmeats with table decorations sculpted in sugar. Part food, part entertainment, a *collazione* was a feature of an important celebration. The idea spread through the European courts, becoming in England a banquet composed of fruit, wine and sweet foods, fashionable during the sixteenth and seventeenth centuries. Relaxed, intimate, fun and frivolous,

Charles Williams, *Dandies Sans-sis-sous*, *c.* 1818, etching, showing the interior of an early 19th-century English sweetshop displaying cakes and jellies as well as candies.

these informal treats were often taken in special rooms or little banqueting houses in gardens. From these precedents, the dessert course of a meal came to consist of sweetmeats – pastry, cakes, fresh or sugar-preserved fruit, macaroons, jellies and marzipan, often further decorated with candies. The word 'sweet' is still sometimes used to refer to items for dessert.

Sweets also developed the diminutive 'sweeties', commonly used for items aimed at small children, and became entangled with the notion of goodness, as in the French *bonbon*, Spanish *bombon* and Portuguese *bombom*, while Dutch *lekker* literally means tasty. Words for sweet things are sometimes subverted by slang for adult concerns relating to drugs and sex, though 'bonbon' still has cachet and implies high-quality candies in North America.

'Lolly', Antipodean English for sweets or candies, originated as an English dialect word for the tongue, surviving in British English as lollipop, a sweet on a stick. In North America these are known as suckers, perhaps with a parallel derivation. In 1862 Henry Weatherley listed dialect terms in England: 'the "Loggets" or "Cushies" of the eastern part of the Kingdom; the "Tom Trot" or "Butter Scotch" of the north; the "Humbugs" or "Lollies" of the south; the Suckers and Hardbake of the west . . .'[2] 'Spice', the local name in parts of Northern England, reflects sugar's former place among exotic imports such as pepper and cinnamon.

The word 'confectionery' ties sweets, candies, chocolate and patisserie together and reflects medieval European attitudes to sugar, when it was perceived as something that enhanced health. From the Latin *conficere*, meaning to put together, the action of compounding, it gave English 'confection' and related words, and the archaic word 'comfit'. French *confiserie*, Italian *confetto* and German *Konfect* share this derivation, and the Spanish buy sweets in a *confitería*.

Originally, 'confection' related to medical uses of sugar, derived from medieval Arabic perceptions of this as a beneficial substance. These were heavily influenced by the doctrine of the four humours, abstract ideas of hot, wet, cold and dry, and associated character types – sanguine, phlegmatic, melancholic and choleric.

> Sugar was regarded as 'hot' and 'moist' . . . Arab apothecaries realized that it was therefore an ideal substance to use as a humoral balance when preparing a drug, either neutralizing 'cold' substances, or warming them up to make them more effective.[3]

The Arabs regarded different forms of sugar as effective for different problems: *sukkar tabarzad abyad*, 'white rock sugar' for bladder, liver and spleen problems; *fanid* for chest pain; and *sukkar abyad*, yet another form of white sugar, was thought good for digestive problems.[4]

The Muslim conquest brought these ideas, and sugar itself, to the Mediterranean, where Venice became especially important in processing it. Confectionery was the province of apothecaries in medieval Europe, and their skills involved working sugar. Vestiges of this can be detected in cough sweets and the words 'pastille', 'lozenge', 'cachou' and 'troche', all of which are used in medicine.

Considered a drug, a spice and a food, many attributes of sugar were useful to the medieval physician. It preserves plant material, can be a vehicle for drugs, and has a pleasant taste that mitigates bitterness. Sugar was hugely expensive in medieval Europe. Novelty and price must have enhanced its status. Apothecaries compounded mixtures to maintain or correct the balance of humours in their patrons, made flavoured syrups and understood distilling, linking confectionery and drinks.

Advertisement for Bonbons Klaus, 1894, lithograph, a typical example of late 19th-century publicity for confectionery.

Paolo Antonio Barbieri, *The Dispensary*, 1637, oil on canvas. Fruit paste in boxes, comfits and gilded leaf-shaped confections are displayed in elaborate jars.

They knew how to cast sugar in moulds, mix malleable pastes for sculptures, and make delicate flour-based items. Flour-based sweet biscuits (cookies), wafers and cakes are still considered confectionery in Europe.

Preservative aspects gave the word *Konditorei* to the German language. Although this now indicates a café serving cakes and desserts, a *Konditor* originally preserved fruit and other items using sugar. Together with the *Zuckerbäcker* (literally 'sugar-baker'), by the eighteenth century they provided all sorts of sweetmeats in the German-speaking world, where a strong guild system influenced the development of confectionery.[5]

The Eastern cultures that originally developed many skills associated with sugar have a less restrictive notion of sweets than modern Western ones. The general term *halva* (transliterated from Arabic and variously spelt *halwa*, *halvah* or *helveh*) simply means sweet and covers many different forms. From a specific sesame-based confection in parts of southeastern Europe, to Indian versions made with lentils or carrots,

> you will find it made with all sorts of ingredients. Flour and semolina 'halvas' are popular from North Africa to Turkey to India and come in many variants . . . presented in various ways, cut into shapes or made into impressively high mounds, artistically decorated with nuts and dried fruit . . .[6]

Recipes for and understanding of halva and its place as a sweetmeat vary widely, giving a plethora of sweet confections, some equivalent to candies or sweets as known in Europe and North America, others pastry- or cookie-like.

Historically, in the Middle East, courts such as that of the Turkish Ottoman Empire supported elaborate social structures of officials, courtiers and soldiers served by craftsmen including *şekerci* (sweet-makers) and *helvasai*, specialist makers of confections. Friedrich Unger, a German confectioner who visited Istanbul in the 1830s, quoted an account of them, fascinating for the numerous divisions: makers of rosewater, buns, wafers, cakes, jelly, almond sweetmeats and a host of other items.[7]

Further east again, categorizing Indian sweets becomes even more difficult. A multiplicity of confections exist, with deep significance in rituals of hospitality, religious performances, festivals and social life. Collective names such as *mithai* (from the Sanskrit word for sweet), *madhur* (from the Sanskrit word for honey) or *mishti* indicate a multitude of flavours and textures: dry, crunchy, fudge-like, soft, milky, juicy, syrupy. Confusingly to the Westerner, salty snacks can be included under these terms. Such foods are categorized as much by

A seller of *laddu* and bright pink cast sugar figures at a Hindu temple in Goa, 1994.

custom as anything else, though there is a general division between 'dry' or 'hard' and 'soft' or 'syrupy' sweetmeats. Ingredients, usage and attitudes relating to sweet foods have elements familiar to Westerners, such as their being snacks, treats or something external to meals, and ones that make them different, such as milk and pulses as ingredients, and the role of sweets in worship or *puja*. They are not exact equivalents of sweets or candies, but have many parallels. Attempting to form categories equivalent to those used in the Western world is futile. Some have resemblances to fudge, marzipan or brittle; others, made from flour or soft unsalted cheese, deep fried and immersed in syrup, are remote from the dry, long-lasting candies and sugar sweets of North America and Europe. The Indian notion of sweet foods is a continuum, its variety reflecting numerous landscapes, climates and cultural practices, and a prolonged history.

Sugar was first extensively refined and used in India, and is deeply embedded in the food cultures of the subcontinent. The origins of many Indian sweetmeats are impossible to disentangle, but sources hint that a tradition of sweets made of flour, butter, milk, sugar and spices was developing by the period AD 600–1200.[8] Ghee and milk products used as ingredients and the complexities of the caste system have given sweet foods a special place. The idea of sweetness is especially important in Bengali culture, giving many idioms to the language. As in European languages, sweetness in flavour is equated with wishes for sweetness in life generally.

Elsewhere in the world, attitudes to sweets and candies vary. They are not absent: Western confectionery companies have ensured that industrially produced versions are available everywhere, and almost all regions have traditional sweet celebratory foods. But the idea of sweets or candy as a long-standing, separate class of foods is, on the whole, less developed and less ubiquitous in areas such as China, Africa and much of Latin America, with certain exceptions.

Both the Spanish and Portuguese left a trail of sweetness around the planet during their explorations. The latter probably influenced Thailand, parts of China, Malaysia, Indonesia, Bengal and Japan, leaving distinctive confections in their wake. Mexico has an interesting and well-developed culture of sweetness, partially derived from Spanish influence. The Philippines, too, drew heavily on Spanish traditions of confectionery, and also twentieth-century North American influence.

Japan has a specific tradition of *wagashi*, which includes confectionery, cakes, cookies and candy, but this is another category that defies translation. According to Richard Hosking, it 'does not correspond to anything in western culture, and can include salty snacks like rice crackers as well'.[9] These have a distinctively Japanese aesthetic, but were developed partly under Chinese influence, with a few detectably European touches. The term is a relatively recent one. Sugar, although known in Japan since sometime in the seventh century, was a precious rarity until the twentieth century and, as in Europe, considered a medicine. The arrival of the Portuguese in the sixteenth century also influenced Japanese sweet foods.

China is often cited as an area with a paucity of sweet foods, especially the intensely sugary types found in the West, but there is evidence that the Chinese are not totally immune to the charms of sugar. A Chinese confectionery tradition probably developed from around the seventh century AD, when sugar began to replace honey in a type of sweet cake. At this time sugar and items made with it were the preserve of the aristocracy, and remained so for several centuries.[10] As elsewhere, sugar fulfilled a variety of purposes – medicine, preservative, flavouring and decorative medium – but it never became a staple food as it did in nineteenth-century Europe and North America, and sweets, candies and sweetened foods in general have remained special-occasion foods.

Sugar is a nutritionally unnecessary but beguiling substance that holds enchantment over certain cultures, especially through the medium of confections. Nutritionists, dentists

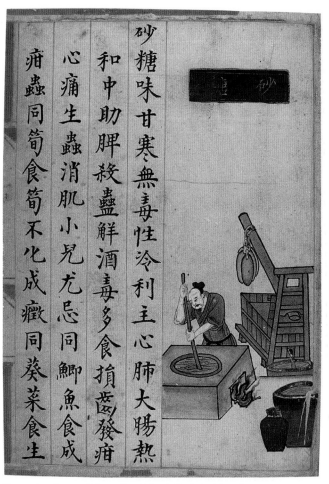

砂糖味甘寒無毒性冷利主心肺大腸熱
和中助脾殺蠱解酒毒多食損齒發疳
心痛生蟲消肌小兒尤忌同鯽魚食成
疳蟲同筍食筍不化成癥同葵菜食生

Illustration from a Chinese 'Food Herbal' of the Ming dynasty
(1368–1644) showing a man preparing granulated sugar from
cane juice. Behind him is a press for extracting cane juice.

Late 19th-century advertisement for Palmer's toffee, one of numerous brands on the market at this time.

and social anthropologists have all puzzled over the reasons behind this, especially in Anglophone cultures. Examining the role of sugar in the diet of the British from the fifteenth century onwards in *Sweetness and Power*, Sidney Mintz considered reasons why it is so appreciated in these islands. These include an inborn liking for sweetness in humans, the original status of sugar as a luxury item, the adoption of bitter drinks such as tea and coffee, sugar as a source of wealth in the seventeenth and eighteenth centuries, the potential sugar has as an ingredient and a decorative medium, and a calorie deficit among the poor during industrialization.

Conspicuous consumption, the idea of a leisured existence, which influenced cakes, pastries and other confections and survives into the modern world despite the availability of cheap sugar and mass-production, has also influenced a desire for sweet things.[11] There are links between childhood pocket money and economic power, and femininity and sweetness. Advertising and marketing have played a significant role since the late nineteenth century. Many people simply enjoy sweets or candies, consumed as humble and inexpensive pleasures, or shared as a gesture of goodwill and friendship.

At the root of notions about sweetness seems to be an equation of sweet equals good: literally, in the sense of tastes good, is good; more abstractly in the idea that sweetness is goodness. Whatever these notions, and however they evolved, they are resistant to the efforts of health educators to persuade people to eat fewer sweets, candies or chocolate bars – though sugar is also ingested in soft drinks, ices, cakes and as an ingredient that, in some form (corn syrup, high-fructose corn syrup, glucose, caramel), is used in numerous manufactured foods. Sugar itself keeps well, but rots teeth. Sweetness is attractive but too much is cloying. Beneath it lies the spectre of slavery, in which millions of Africans were forcibly transported to work in brutal conditions on West Indian sugar plantations, all to supply a growing market for sugar in Europe and North America.

Confections are ambiguous. Sweets, candies, confections, bonbons – whatever they are called – are highly visible and unnecessary manifestations of sugar, qualities that probably also play a large part in their attraction. Ephemeral, intended to be eaten, they store well. They can be admired for beauty and novelty, brought out for special occasions. Portable, they make ideal gifts. Working sugar is technically demanding and uses luxury ingredients. Sugar preserves fruit, nuts and flavours – and shapes ideas and aspirations long after the original significance has been lost.

2
The Magic of Sugar

The sparkling transparent sweets and candies of the traditional confectioner's shop are made by sugar boiling, a technique that produces some of the most eye-catching and nostalgia-ridden items. The skill has been most energetically exploited in Western Europe and North America, but there is some knowledge of it wherever sugar is used. 'Boiled goods', a confectioner's term, is wide and inclusive: 'it embraces drops, rocks, candies, toffees, caramels, creams . . .'[1]

One might pause, and ask why honey is not made into confectionery. In sixteenth-century Europe it was clarified, boiled and manipulated in some recipes, as recorded by Michel de Nostradamus. The tradition has vanished, though honey-based confectionery survived into the nineteenth century in Turkey. Honey, however, has strong flavours; supply is limited, and it has a different chemistry to sugar. The latter is easy to work and is cheap and abundant.

Fruit juices, such as *dibs* (boiled date juice) and *pekmez* (boiled grape juice), also provide sweetness in the Middle East, but are expensive, strongly flavoured and less easy to manipulate. Indians use *gur*, sugar from date palm sap: variable in colour, with smoky, sour and bitter notes, this is valued for flavour. Malt sugar, from sprouting grain, has been used in China for millennia. In North America, maple sap gives distinctively flavoured but expensive syrup and candy.

Partially refined sugars and refinery by-products have limited applications, often for flavour. Jaggery (brown sugar produced locally from cane) is used in India. Golden syrup, black treacle and molasses are added to some confections in Britain and North America where they aid flavour and texture, while invoking nostalgia for a simpler past when they were widely used for cheap candy.

Sugar is essential to confectionery. It was relatively easy to control, and could be refined to pure white, desirable qualities in places such as late medieval Venice, vital in the transmission of both sugar and skills in working it from the Arab world to northwest Europe. Initial classifications of sugar as a spice and a medicine and its power as sweetener and preservative placed it in the province of apothecaries, who had a close association with refining and selling it. Venetian

Making jaggery, coarse brown sugar, in Pune, India. Lumps of jaggery probably provided the earliest sugar sweets, but it had to be further refined to produce white sugar suitable for fine confectionery.

De Suikerbacker.

In Christi Bloed,   Lach God'lyk Soet.

Die 't wrange Zuur wil overwinnen
Moet met geen Aquafort beginnen,
   Maar Suiker is het rechte Swaard:
ôGod! hoe hebd ghy 't Suure Leeven,
Uw hoogste Soetheid in gegeeven,
   En soo, de groote Val herbaard.

In Jan Luyken's 1694 etching *De Suikerbacker*, a refiner or a journeyman confectioner carries a loaf of refined sugar.

cane plantations on Mediterranean islands, notably Cyprus, generated enormous wealth, and Italy, with a culture of conspicuous display among the aristocracy, provided patrons and an audience for the products. Large numbers of apothecaries in sixteenth-century Venice and guild restrictions regulating price may have led to a need to differentiate products, establishing a theme of innovation which has persisted in European and North American confectionery.

In sugar boiling, a notion of different 'stages', observable in syrups as they cook, is an essential concept. Full codification of this took several centuries. Before boiling commenced, sugar needed clarifying, by dissolving it in water and adding egg whites. On heating, these formed a scum that was lifted off, leaving a limpid syrup. Historic recipes, therefore, begin with prepared syrup, unlike modern ones which specify quantities of sugar and water. This, and the archaic terms contained in historic recipes, make them obscure. Seventeenth-century English texts talk of 'candy height', 'sugar boiled to sugar again' and 'Manus Christi height' – the latter especially confusing, as Manus Christi was at one point small pieces of sugar mixed with gold leaf, at another a rose- or violet-flavoured cordial. By the early eighteenth century, boiling stages showed more codification. Syrups were closely observed: did they boil with pearl-like bubbles, or make feather-like strands when shaken off a skimmer? An early system was published in France by La Varenne (1661), and in English by John Nott in his *Cooks and Confectioners Dictionary* (1726). Joseph Gilliers in *Le Cannameliste français* (1751) gave a more detailed description of stages and their associated tests. Gradually various terms and systems of observation were codified into the system now generally recognized. Their names and temperatures are as follows:[2]

Thread: 215–35°F / 102–13°C
Soft ball: 235–40°F / 113–16°C
Hard ball: 240–65°F / 121–30°C
Crack (or soft crack): 270–90°F / 132–43°C
Hard crack: 300–310°F / 149–54°C

In the past, hard crack was called caramel, a name now given to sugar a few degrees beyond this temperature, when it starts to break down and brown. This was considered spoilt in the past, perhaps because it could not be recycled. Sugar finally burns at 205°C (400°F).

Hydrometers, thermometers and industrial machinery, along with cheap, pure, industrially refined sugar, available from the mid-nineteenth century onwards, made sugar boiling into a factory process. Science also unravelled details. Each molecule of sucrose (ordinary white sugar) consists of one molecule each of two smaller sugar molecules, fructose and glucose. This gives distinct physical properties exploited by

Two men stirring sugar syrup in pans at Barratt's Confectionery Works in Wood Green, London, in 1946.

confectioners. Dissolved in water, solid white sugar becomes a clear syrup through inversion, as the bonds between fructose and glucose break. All crystals must be dissolved before boiling starts, as any remaining in the syrup provide a template and can induce re-crystallization during boiling. Heating syrup evaporates water at boiling point (100°C/212°F). Continued boiling evaporates more water, leaving an increasingly concentrated syrup, which is supersaturated (the higher temperature allows water to hold more sugar in solution than the same amount can hold at room temperature). Thin and runny at just above 100°C, syrup becomes thicker and more malleable at higher temperatures until all but a tiny percentage of the water has evaporated.

Slow cooling and stirring the syrup allow the fructose and glucose to re-crystallize as sucrose. In the language of confectioners, they 'grain', becoming an opaque crystalline solid. Swift cooling of concentrated syrup maintains inversion in the mixture, and the sugar forms a clear, glass-like solid at room temperature. The boiling temperature window of 100–150°C (122–302°F), and the phenomena of inversion and re-crystallization, are the basis of the sugar boiler's craft.

Control is essential. Confectioners add ingredients which affect sugar chemistry: tartaric or other acids, molasses, golden syrup, black treacle and honey all alter relative proportions of glucose and fructose in sugar syrup, preventing it fully re-crystallizing. Corn (glucose) syrup, developed in the nineteenth century, and high-fructose corn syrup, further processed with enzymes to convert glucose into fructose (a product of the mid-twentieth century), also act this way and are essential to industrial confectionery manufacture. Called 'doctors' by generations of confectioners, they are now known as interfering agents. Dairy produce, fats and oils, which interfere physically with graining, are used in some confections.

Rock candy, in large, transparent, sparkling crystals, is perhaps the most elemental confection, with at least a thousand years of history. Described in medieval Arabic, it was known as *qand* or *sukkar nabat*, and deposited on sticks.[3] It was also known in China. By the sixteenth century it was widely known in Europe, grown on sticks or strings in containers of syrup kept warm for about a week in low steady heat.

George Flegel, *Still-life with Bread and Sweetmeats*, first half of the 17th century, oil painting showing a bowl of comfits, pears encrusted with candied sugar and a heart-shaped confection.

When the container was drained and opened, the crystals were revealed. Other sweetmeats could also be candied by this method.

In the late nineteenth century the process was routinely used both in Europe and North America to give items such as fondants and fruit jellies a sparkling surface that resisted humidity. Rock candy is still produced, left in a warm room at 49°C (120°F) for forty hours. Into the 1950s the process retained a kind of magic, and one North American confectionery manual suggested the waste candy, re-dissolved, could be sold as 'rock candy syrup'.[4] From New Year celebrations in Afghanistan, to coffee stirrers in the most fashionable metropolitan coffee bars, this ancient form of candy still has a place: 'a testament to the power of sweetness that . . . the simplest sweet of all remained popular for about 900 years after it was introduced to northern Europe'.[5]

Another form of candy consists of amorphous masses of small crystals (as seen in sugar loaves), made by pouring syrup into fancy moulds. The method, known for centuries, was described in modern terms in the late nineteenth century when E. Skuse explained how to cast small novelties, including graining the sugar:

> Boil sufficient sugar . . . to the degree of ball, 250 [Fahrenheit] by thermometer; remove it from the fire and rub the sugar against the side of the pan until thick and white; stir all together then fill the moulds . . . [6]

Moulded cast sugar has a depth and spread of history comparable with that of rock candy, with mentions from tenth-century Egypt and twelfth-century China. There was a trade in such items: 'Medieval China enjoyed sweets made from cane sugar boiled in milk, some of them shaped into figurines

One half of a plaster mould for casting a Sicilian *pupa de cena*, a sugar image made for All Souls' Day at the start of November.

such as lions. Making these for the Chinese market was a speciality, apparently, of both Sichuan and of distant Persia.'[7]

Moulded sugar 'in the shapes of foreign pagodas, people, birds, and animals' is known to have been used at various ceremonies in seventeenth-century Kuang-Tung province in China.[8] In Europe cast sugar made subtleties, ornamental and entertaining figures for medieval feasts, and novelties for the collazione and sugar banquets of the sixteenth and seventeenth centuries. In 1609, Sir Hugh Plat instructed how 'To mold of a lemmon, orange, peare, Nut, &c. and after to cast it hollow within, of sugar' by making a plaster mould first.[9] A pig's foot could be cast this way, an example of the jokiness that often accompanies sugar, echoed in nineteenth-century cast-sugar 'fancies' for Christmas. These included pigs' heads, violins, slippers, dogs, cats and rabbits, and sold for a penny or less.[10] By this time a novel technique known as starch moulding was used for small, uniform items. Plaster shapes are used to make impressions in trays of starch, filled with liquid syrup and left undisturbed. The starch draws moisture from the syrup, helping the candy set.

Cast sugar was evidently irresistible, and survives with a patchy but wide distribution. It forms Mexican sugar skulls for *Todos Santos* (All Saints), ornamented with brilliantly coloured icing and paper, and Sicilian *pupi di cena*, sugar images, often of knights on horseback, for the same festival and for Easter. It can be found in the seafront shops of the British Isles, in Cairo and at the festival of Diwali in India.

There are softer-grained confections. The confectioner Friedrich Unger, visiting Istanbul in the 1830s, described a candy new to him, the soft-textured *lohuk scherbet*, and he speculated about it as a novelty to introduce on his return to Europe. History does not record if he did so, and the French are credited with introducing fondant (from *fondre*, to melt), or 'soft rich eating candies called "creams" which are of recent introduction' to European confectionery in the mid-nineteenth century.[11] Whoever was responsible, their unctuous texture is quite unlike the resilient, hard snap of cast sugar.

Syrup for fondant is boiled to a relatively low temperature, cooled somewhat, and then worked intensively. Cooler syrup means less energy in the mix, and working prevents fructose and glucose re-bonding, creating numerous microscopic crystals suspended in liquid syrup. Imperceptible when eaten, these give the overall impression of smoothness. Corn syrup aids production of small crystals and is routinely added to fondant. Invertase, an enzyme added to the mixture before it is sealed in a chocolate case, partially inverts some of the sugar back to glucose and fructose to give a magically soft-textured filling.

Late nineteenth-century technology produced novel flavouring essences and dyes; combined with starch-moulded

An 1880s advertisement for McCobbs Owl brand Chocolate Creams. Confections with chocolate coatings and fondant centres were enormously popular in the late 19th century.

fondant, these allowed production of an apparently infinite range of candies and bonbons. Eating chocolate, developed in the first half of the nineteenth century, provided an interesting, bitter contrast in flavour. When eaten, the confections melted at roughly the same temperature and rate, a luxurious sensation on the palate. Fondant filled the first chocolate candy bars, Chocolate Cream, devised by Fry's in 1866. Initially bonbons were hand-dipped, but by 1900 enrobing machines conveyed the centres through curtains of molten chocolate. Fondant still fills chocolates and after-dinner mints and makes realistic whites and yolks in Easter eggs, especially the Cadbury Creme Egg, an iconic Easter treat of British childhoods. As *szaloncuckor* (literally 'parlour candy'), chocolate-covered fondants wrapped in glittery paper decorate Christmas trees in Hungary and Slovakia.

Fondant itself is added to other confections, especially fudge, to induce crystallization and control texture. Fudge has complex and attractive flavours, distinctive toasty-caramel notes, derived from dairy produce cooked with sugar. Obscure in origin, it enjoyed a vogue in late nineteenth-century America: 'From its first appearance in newspapers, magazines, cookbooks and advertising pamphlets in the 1880s, fudge was promoted to the home cook and amateur candy maker as an innocent pleasure suitable for the domestic environment.'[12]

The name may relate to cobbling together – fudging – something. More importantly, it was an immediate success, with a wholesome, homespun image. In the USA, making it became a fad at women's colleges and a pastime at children's parties. The technique of graining commercially made fudge by adding fondant is mentioned as early as 1912.[13] Extreme climate may have played a part in its popularity; in the 1950s commercial confectioners in the USA thought it an ideal substitute for chocolates, which melted in the summer heat.

Fudge rapidly became popular in the rest of the English-speaking world. Chocolate was always a favourite flavour. Vanilla, nuts, maple syrup, liqueurs, fruit essences and combinations such as rum and raisin appear, altering with fashion. Simple to make, with a relatively low capital input, it is a confection whose manufacture was successfully franchised in small shops in tourist locations in the last few decades of the twentieth century.

Two highly localized milk and sugar confections still made in Europe might have influenced its development; they belong to Scotland and to the Netherlands. Scottish tablet, sugar and milk or cream boiled together and grained by beating, may sound similar to fudge but is subtly different, with a crisper initial texture, dissolving swiftly through a pleasing slurry of small crystals when eaten. A degree or two in boiling temperature and a plainer mix makes the difference. Originally the name described the flat shape, and recipes for 'tablets' flavoured with ginger, orange or rose are given in 1736 in the earliest printed Scottish cookery book, *Mrs McLintock's Receipts for Cookery and Pastry-work*. Dutch *borstplaat* is another candied confection; *borst* means chest, and it was originally made and sold by apothecaries as a remedy for respiratory ailments. Modern varieties are a mixture of cream and sugar, made into a thin sheet or poured in moulds, traditional to early December around St Nicholas's Day.[14]

Other tourist souvenirs are based on grained candies. New Orleans pralines, sold both from shops and by *pralinières*, the (usually female) makers on street corners in the city, are large drops of grained sugar boiled with milk, butter or cream, mixed with chopped pecans. In 1893, 'prawleens' were described as a mixture of New Orleans molasses, brown sugar, chocolate and butter.[15] 'Delicious pink and white sugar cakes made of coconut and sugar' and 'brown ones made

New Orleans *pralinière* with her basket of sugar and nut confections.

of pecans and sugar' were mentioned under the heading 'pralines' in *The Picayune's Creole Cookbook* in 1901.

'Praline' is a French word, and pralines as made in France are hard textured, made from unblanched almonds tumbled in caramelized sugar, a technique known as *sablage*. There are numerous varieties, one of which is said to have originated in the household of the Comte du Plessis-Praslin in the seventeenth century. Whatever their origin, they were widely known. In 1820, in *The Italian Confectioner*, William Jarrin commented that *prawlings* were covered in dry sugar to preserve them from moisture; he enumerates pistachio, orange flowers and almonds in white or red versions. The Spanish make *garrapiñadas*, which seem more or less identical. Confusingly, Belgian pralines are chocolates, originally named from the toasted nut and sugar mixtures, ground up for flavouring.

The 'pink and white sugar cakes' of coconut, mentioned in New Orleans, recall coconut ice, a confection which suddenly appears in British confectionery books towards the end of the nineteenth century, made with grained sugar and freshly grated coconut, soon replaced with desiccated coconut. In North America in the 1950s, coconut candies were a popular year-round confection. They became the filling for favourites such as Mound, first produced by the U.S. company Hershey in 1921, and Bounty, first produced by Mars Inc., in the early 1950s (still available in the UK, Canada and Australia, and elsewhere). Perhaps coconut and sugar is an obvious combination, wherever the two are available. Candied coconut sweets are traditional in Mexico, Brazil, the West Indies, Southeast Asia and India.

Maple candy owes nothing to cane. It is made in eastern Canada and the northeastern USA from maple sap collected in early spring. High in sugars, concentrated by boiling, it is poured into moulds to set, giving little candies with a fudge-like texture, or poured onto snow to chill it quickly as maple taffy. Native American populations tapped maple and other trees for sap, though opinions vary over the extent to which they boiled syrup or sugar before settlers of European origin took up the process.[16] Whatever the truth, maple is a

NANE LİMONLU AKİDE
(WITH MINT AND LEMON)
18,00TL

SUSAMLI AKİDE
(WITH SESAME)
18,00TL

sought-after flavour used in many confections and candies,
especially with pecans and walnuts.

Where, in this plethora of opaque and variously hard-
textured or creamy candies, are the innumerable transparent
and striped confections? Their jewelled colours and myriad
shapes fill the jars in the 'traditional' confectionery shops
of nostalgic imagination, the boiled sweets of Britain and

Boiled and flavoured sugar drops, *akide*, displayed in traditional glass jars in Istanbul, 2012.

hard candy of North America. Where are the ancestors of fruit-drop Lifesavers, Fox's Glacier Mints, pear drops?

Such sweets are simple in principle. Syrup boiled to hard crack and cooled quickly gives their sparkling transparency. To aid this, confectioners 'cut the grain', or 'greased' the sugar, using various 'doctors' or interfering agents. Lemon juice or honey were used in a pre-industrial age; glucose or tartaric acid in mass production, further inhibiting crystallization. This gives a material with much creative potential. While still warm and malleable, the mixture can be worked, moulded, cut into smaller pieces or even blown like glass.

Before the nineteenth century, a handful of recipes appeared. Most eighteenth-century English cookbooks contain recipes for clear barley sugar, sugar boiled to crack, cut in sticks or tablets. An early nineteenth-century observer, Friedrich Unger, noted hard-boiled sweets wrapped in papers in Istanbul, calling them *papillottes*. This term implies that he already associated such sweets or their presentation with France. Then the British took to boiled sugar sweets in all their sparkling glory, and consumption of these increased until Henry Weatherley wrote in 1865 that 'beyond question . . . the English people prefer boiled sugars, as the simplest and most genuine sweets'.[17] His book was published in Philadelphia, so he may have helped to popularize them in North America.

The Great Exhibition of 1851 in London had popularized many manufactured goods, including confectionery. Before this, Weatherley asserted, boiled sweets 'were almost exclusively an English manufacture' but

> the introduction therein of the author's and other English confectioners' goods, and also the machines, led to their manufacture by other nations, the German confectioners in particular, and as regards variety or skill, they are not likely to be surpassed.[18]

Half a century later, E. Skuse considered that at least two-thirds of confectionery made in Britain consisted of boiled sugar.[19] The French called such sweets caramels (they are still called *caramelo* in Spanish and *karamel* in Russian, a reflection of the earlier use of the word to indicate hard crack by confectioners).

Boiled sugar sweets became ever cheaper and more attractive. Sugar was a diminishing part of the total cost. Instant energy from cheap sweets, combined with colourful, varied shapes and flavours, was welcome in the intense poverty of

Late 19th-century drop rollers stored in a rack on the wall of a confectioner's boiling room.

industrial cities in Britain and elsewhere. Perhaps even the cost of coal was influential, as boiling sugar is a fuel-hungry process.

Originally boiled sugar was simply dropped on paper or formed into small sticks. Machines introduced speed and shape. Working by hand, a skilled sugarworker and a boy could boil and shape 3 kg of sugar in thirty minutes. The introduction in 1847 of drop rollers meant that a boy alone could make the same quantity in five minutes. Drop rollers were developed by Oliver Chase, in Boston, Massachusetts, and swiftly became indispensable. Still used, these are paired rollers engraved with patterns. Boiled sugar syrup, cooled to a malleable temperature, is fed through them and impressed with three-dimensional shapes. The new industrial flavours and colours displaced traditional fruit juices, spices, rosewater and plant-derived pigments such as saffron, originally used with boiled sugar.

Shapes became ever more fantastical: animals, flowers, stars, acorns, nuts, fish, scissors, frogs, seashells, shamrocks and Santa Claus and turkeys for Christmas. Catalogues such as those of Thomas Mills and Brother, a Chicago company, display multifarious designs. 'Cheap, brightly coloured, fanciful pieces of hard-boiled sugar, penny candies enchanted children, who saw them as dazzling gemstones in the glass jars of the corner store.'[20] Larger versions became the clear sugar toys, traditional Christmas gifts for youngsters in North America. What child could resist a candy figure of a person being butted by a goat, a man trapped by a dog pulling at his coat, a monkey eating fruit, a camel or an elephant?

These formed another chapter in the use of sugar to make extraordinary shapes. Other cultures had sugar fantasies as well: a traditional street entertainment in Japan, *amezaiku*, consists of sculpting shapes including flowers and animals from molten sugar. China has similar traditions, including making

PATTERNS OF TOYS
MADE BY MILLS' EXCELSIOR TOY MACHINE

Thirty-three different patterns, with perfectly flat bases. They will stand erect.
Varying from 25 to 40 to the pound.

A 1930s catalogue for Thomas Mills and Brother of Philadelphia, manufacturers of confectioners' machinery and tools; this page shows patterns for sugar toys.

pictures by tracing them on a board with molten sugar, and blowing malt sugar syrup as if it were molten glass. Their history is unclear but their hold over children of all ages is plain to see.

Older confections survived alongside novelties. Barley sugar, applied to high-boiled sugar in the nineteenth century, was originally sugar boiled with a decoction of barley instead of plain water, as was *sucre d'orge* in France. Barley is still used in *sucre d'orge de religieuses de Moret*, a speciality of Moret sur Loing.

Barley sugar is not such a simple subject as it appears. In English, until the early twentieth century, it was sometimes equated with confections called pennets, short sticks of sugar, sometimes rendered opaque and white by a technique known as pulling, and considered good for colds. Both the word and the quality of whiteness hint at forms of sugar known in the

A candy maker manipulates a rope of sugar by pulling, stretching and folding, Xian, China, 2016. This process, although not well recorded, is of ancient origin.

Pulling sugar by machine, safer but less spectacular than traditional hand crafting.

past, and link such novelties as candy canes back to the cold cures of the ancient world.

Pulling sugar uses syrup boiled to crack. When cool enough to handle but still malleable, the mass is intensively worked. Today this takes a few seconds on a machine with rotating arms, but was formerly done by hand, the mass thrown over an iron hook and stretched and folded. It soon turns white: the process forms tiny sugar crystals and incorporates pockets of air, the mixture becoming 'many fine, partly crystalline strands separated by columns of air, a combination that becomes a solid fabric of shiny threads'.[21]

Some of the most beautiful and eye-catching confectionery is produced this way. Candy canes of North American Christmases, with red and white spiralling their length, British seaside rock with the name of the resort mysteriously running through a stick of white sugar, Scottish 'boilings', multicoloured and striped, which make a fine display in ranks of jars on the sweetshop shelves, and French *berlingots*, little coloured sweets striped with satiny white sugar, a speciality of the town of Carpentras, as well as intriguing chalky textured candies and fine, floss-like sugar strands all owe their form to this skill.

Pulling sugar is an ancient technique, possibly one that was originally considered to confer special qualities. Investigating the word 'pennet' reveals an unexpected depth of history beneath a glittery surface of nineteenth-century industrialization. Like 'candy', and the word 'sugar' itself, 'pennet' hints at the high value placed on sucrose over distance and time. It is 'an anglicized version of the medieval Latin *penidium* . . . from the Arabic *al-fanid*, an expression recorded in thirteenth-century Moslem Spain, meaning pulled sugar shaped into rings and discs'.[22] *Alfeñique* (Spanish) and *alfenim* (Portuguese) both share this derivation and denote sugar worked until white (though the words seem better remembered in colonial situations – Mexico, Bolivia, the Azores – than in Iberia). *Fânîd* was borrowed into Arabic from Persian, in turn probably taken from the Sanskrit word *phanita* to describe specific forms of semi-refined sugar. According to the medieval Arab physician Ibn al-Quff (1233–1286), *fânîd* 'is effective against chest pain and calms one's nerves by reducing cold substances in the chest'.[23]

This ascribed property accompanied pulled sugar on its westward journey. Michel de Nostradamus gave a recipe in 1552, with details showing the process was well understood.

'Wind it or spin it thickly or thinly and daintily, as you will.' Honey or oil discoloured the sugar and made it keep badly. 'The result . . . instead of alleviating the pain of a sore throat, makes it burn far worse.'[24] In the early nineteenth century, pulled sugar had apparently become a downmarket item, in Italy the province of street confectioners. Likewise, Henry Weatherley, on a visit to Paris in 1848, found only one example of common boiled sweets, boiled over charcoal on an open-air stall, and pulled until white.

Cultures have taken the technique and played with it by adding stripes and patterns. Candy canes and other striped pulled sugar sweets are made from a cylinder of white pulled sugar striped with lengths of plain boiled sugar, traditionally red, which are pulled out again to the required thickness and cut into short lengths (as is *polkargris*, a sweet associated with Gränna in Sweden). Peppermint oil is the usual flavouring, although anise, clove and other essences are used, sometimes with different colour combinations.

Juan van der Hamen y León, *Table with Basket of Confectionery*, 1620, oil on canvas. Among the candied fruit and biscuits are two white twisted confections, possibly made from pulled sugar.

British seaside rock was called motto rock when it was first produced. To make it, lengths of coloured sugar are formed into slabs and cylinders – for example, a cylinder of white sugar wrapped in red forms the letter 'O' when seen in section. The elements are built up into a large conical mass, which is spun out and chopped crosswise, leaving the pattern evident in the cut ends of each portion. The sugar must be kept warm during working, as it has to be malleable for pulling and shaping.[25]

Evidence points towards the trick of adding letters as a mid-nineteenth-century novelty developed in London. Henry Mayhew, in *London Labour and the London Poor*, was apparently the first person to record it, and Henry Weatherley commented on 'the beautiful variety of rocks and sticks, both striped and plain' and LOVE rock, seemingly the collective name at the time.[26] Simple sounding, the process required skill and observation of detail for excellent results. The custom of adding letters seems to be a British one, but complex patterns were (and still are) made elsewhere.

Bullseyes and humbugs, smaller striped sweets regarded as 'traditional' in Britain, probably evolved during the same period. Cheap and eye-catching, they flooded the market, together with transparent sweets, especially in towns. On both sides of the Atlantic pulled sugar sweets are considered inconsequential but pretty. Hugely attractive, they held a fascination for many observers, and were often remembered from childhood, sometimes as humble trivialities, sometimes as novelties for festive occasions.

Some traditional pulled sweets still demand a further process of maturing or graining (grained sugar is less likely to become sticky in uncertain storage conditions), such as toothachingly sweet Edinburgh rock, chalky pastel-coloured sticks named for the Scottish capital. Myth attributes the process to

Seafront stall selling seaside rock, confectionery and other items, UK, 2016.

accidental discovery but similar confections exist elsewhere. Dutch *kaneel-brokken*, cinnamon-coloured and flavoured, and harder than Edinburgh rock, shares the grained texture, as does Turkish *peynir şekeri* (literally, sugar cheese). Friedrich Unger observed that the latter was consumed

> in great quantities in the Orient . . . This pulled sugar the Turk produces with great dexterity and during the preparation lends to them all imaginable varieties of colour and shapes . . . There is no difference between the method of preparation used here and the European.[27]

The mixture was flavoured with vanilla, rose, orange, cinnamon or other essences.

Another pulled sugar sweet made in Turkey is one of the most extraordinary of confections. Known as *keten helva*, or *pişmâniye*, this has a thistledown, filament-like texture derived from a combination of technique and ingredients. A mixture

Making dragon's beard candy (closely related to *pişmâniye*) by pulling sugar syrup into a mass of fine threads.

of butter and flour is cooked and stirred together for almost an hour, while a sugar syrup is prepared, boiled to crack, pulled until white and shaped into a ring.

> The pulled sugar ring is generously sprinkled with roasted flour and placed in the centre of a large circular tray. Three, four or more people sit around the tray, place both hands on the ring, and squeeze it, simultaneously moving it in an anti-clockwise direction. This requires a flawless rhythmic movement so that the ring does not become thinner in some parts and eventually break.[28]

The ring expands and is folded back on itself, sprinkled with more flour, an action repeated at least ten times. At each fold the strands become thinner, eventually achieving the curious floss-like texture. The technique has been known for over five centuries in Turkey, and the alternative name, *pişmâniye*, derives from the Persian *pashm*, wool, hinting at a wider knowledge of this sweetmeat. The extent of knowledge about pulled sugar in the Far East in early times is obscure, but observations made in the market places of Kuang Tang (modern Guangdong) in China in the seventeenth century speak of 'cocoon sugar' and sugar boiled down and made into delicate threads, as well as blown sugar.[29]

There is no equivalent to *keten helva* in Western confectionery. Candyfloss, or cotton candy, made by spinning sugar crystals off a hot surface, is coarse and gritty in texture and has none of the finesse of *keten helva*. The process has been partially mechanized, but pulling is still done by hand. A true test of skill, it was often made at home, and *helva* parties in Turkey were once a feature of winter evenings.

In North America, pulling sugar at 'taffy pulls' became a fashionable social event and entertainment for children around 1900. Taffy making also became a commercial enterprise, and it was made on seaside boardwalks as an attraction. Saltwater taffy, now made in numerous colours and flavours, each nugget wrapped in waxed paper, developed as a peculiarly North American form. Like many candies, it has an invention myth associated with it, relating to the contamination of a batch of taffy with seawater in the 1880s. A more likely explanation is that sellers of the candy 'simply liked the name and its association with seaside pleasures, and began using it to sell their taffy'.[30] Perhaps cheap trips to the seaside, requiring souvenirs, were the important factor; British seaside rock is first recorded around the same time. Industrial formulae for saltwater taffy in the 1950s contained minute amounts of salt, a teaspoonful for about 11 kg of other ingredients, and were lightened with marshmallow whip, a concoction of sugar, corn syrup, albumen and gelatine.

North American 'taffy' indicates various forms of chewy candy, distinguished by an absence of dairy ingredients, the mass pulled to lighten both colour and texture. Soft and chewy, it bears no apparent relation to toffee as understood in modern Britain, which in modern practice is not usually pulled and (supposedly) contains butter, milk or cream. These prevent graining and react with hot sugar to form the toasty, nutty flavours that are so attractive in these sweets.

Dolle's Candyland in Rehoboth Beach, Delaware, is a family business that has been selling saltwater taffy and other homemade candy since 1927.

Strawberry-banana flavour saltwater taffy, one of 94 flavours on sale in Seaside, Oregon, in 2016.

The origins of North American taffy and British toffee are mixed up in the boiling pans of the past. No Arabic origin can be claimed for the names. In Scottish dialect, *taffie* denoted treacle and flour boiled together for Halloween. *Tafia*, in the eighteenth century a molasses-based alcoholic drink, suggests a possible origin. Molasses or treacle went into cheap confections made by street sellers in the nineteenth century, when dialect words included 'the far-famed "Toffee" . . . we find it a great favourite wherever introduced'.[31] 'Toffee' was also confectioner's jargon, used by sugar boilers for syrups boiled to hard crack.

A kind of confectioner's bat-and-ball exchange of recipes took place over the North Atlantic. North Americans make something called 'English toffee' (confusingly for the English, for whom toffee is just toffee). Hard, buttery, studded with almonds and little made in England, this is probably an inheritance from English almond rock and almond hardbake, brown sugar boiled to crack and combined in various ways with almonds, mentioned by Henry Mayhew as a popular street seller's confection in 1864.

'American caramels' or 'Philadelphia caramels' arrived in Britain in the late nineteenth century to an enthusiastic welcome. These confections were of sugar, milk and various fats, butter and cream (or items of non-dairy origin). Recipes were sought after, one commercial confectioner remarking that he went to much trouble and paid a significant sum of money to acquire one.[32] One of his recipes includes sugar, cream, glucose and butter, boiled to crack and flavoured with vanilla. Caramels, Charles Appell noted in the 24 pages of recipes he devoted to them in 1912, should be chewy, and these probably were.

They arrived in a country where toffee was a confection with a delicious buttery flavour and a crisp, hard snap, such as Everton toffee (from Everton, now a suburb of Liverpool) and Doncaster butterscotch, both developed in the early to mid-nineteenth century. In Halifax in Yorkshire around 1900 John Mackintosh developed a new, chewy toffee combining the flavour of toffee and the texture of North American caramels. In turn he took this to the USA, advertising it with overflowing self-assurance:

> I am John Mackintosh, the Toffee King, Sovereign of Pleasure, Emperor of Joy. My old English candy tickles my millions of subjects. My Court Jester's name is Appetite . . . I am the world's largest consumer of butter, my own herd of prize cattle graze the Yorkshire hills. I buy sugar by the trainload. I am John Mackintosh, Toffee King of England and I rule alone.[33]

Despite this, North Americans might argue for the chewy caramel-chocolate mixture of Tootsie Rolls (devised in 1896) as the real inspiration for chewy toffee.

Caramels, notoriously sticky, welded the jaws of generations of schoolchildren together while influencing British ideas of what toffee should be like. Numerous companies took up the confection: Sharps, who made 'kreemy' toffee; Parkinson's, Keiller's or Callard & Bowser for butterscotch; Farrahs, Bluebird, Thorntons and many more. Brand guaranteed quality, for, as E. Skuse remarked about caramels, 'When first brought over from America these goods were certainly a treat . . . Very soon the demand was universal, competition stepped in . . . the prices were lowered, the quality suffered.'[34]

Old-fashioned unbranded toffee was still made both at home and by small local confectioners. A mixture of sugar, treacle and milk or butter boiled together, it was poured into trays to set. The vendor, often in some local general store, broke it into hard, brittle chips using a special toffee hammer, a tradition that lasted well into the 1970s. In my Yorkshire childhood, this was an essential part of mid-autumn, around Halloween and on 5 November, Guy Fawkes Night.

Toffee benefited from developments in marketing, a skill refined and exploited for chocolate. This, the product of developments made by nineteenth-century entrepreneurs in Britain, France, Switzerland and the USA, was produced as tablets or used to enrobe other confections, then packed in foil and pretty wrappers or boxes and promoted as a luxurious gift. Toffee was cheaper, but came in decorative and useful tins (airtight packaging was essential, as it easily became sticky), suitable for gifts and special occasions, helping to promote brands and enhancing their status.

Another innovation was the notion of the countline, bars sold by number, not weight, often coated in chocolate.

Advertisement for Sharp's Toffee, 1924. Toffee, heavily publicized and enormously popular, was exported all over the world, especially to countries of the British Empire.

When manufacturers on both sides of the Atlantic began experimenting with these, they used other confections as fillings. Caramel was a popular choice, along with nougat, mallow, crisped rice and peanuts. Hard-boiled sugar confectionery was less popular, as the texture does not blend as well, though tiny chips can add crunch and flavour. In Britain caramel is consumed daily in the form of Mars Bars (devised in 1932), an item absent from those produced in the USA – there, instead, the Mars company put it into Snickers (devised in 1930).[35]

Honeycomb toffee, frothed by adding bicarbonate of soda to the boiling mass, is also familiar to consumers as the centre of Crunchie bars (Cadbury, marketed through many Commonwealth countries) or Violet Crumble (Nestlé, sold in Australia and New Zealand). Originally this was an eye-catching local novelty. In Ireland, a pulled version, yellowman, is associated with Lammas (summer) fairs and a similar recipe was mentioned in *The Picayune's Creole Cookbook* as *candi tiré à la melasse*, a Louisiana speciality. In America it is known as sponge candy, or seafoam; in New Zealand as hokey-pokey; and in Spain it is coloured black and known as *carbón* (coal), and is given to naughty children.

A scatter of more individual confections are found in other countries. Crisp, buttery, and to British palates butter-scotch-like, Werther's Original, made by Storck, a company founded in Germany in 1903, is one successful brand. Christmas in Sweden brings *knäck*, sugar, cream, syrup and almonds boiled to textures varying from soft and fudge-like to chewy. 'Knäck' can also be used to mean crack, suggesting a distant link with high-boiled sugar.

Salty notes (as in the current fad for salted caramel) are sometimes involved: Dutch *boterbabbelaars* are a mixture of butter, sugar, dark treacle and vinegar with the addition of a little salt. The name is untranslatable – 'its component parts simply mean "butter" and "chatterbox'" – but no one ever said that confectionery followed logical rules.[36] Coffee, too, is a popular flavour. Dutch *Haagsche Hopjes* are said to have been invented by Baron Henrik Hop, a Netherlands diplomat with gout and a taste for coffee. Spanish *dos cafes*, little squares of chewy caramel, might have a distant relationship with the creamy, chewy coffee bomboons whose recipe was published in the eighteenth century by Borella, confectioner to the Spanish ambassador. None of these has the collective identities of toffee in the English-speaking world, and their distant origins remain a mystery; but toffee, caramel and butterscotch have escaped the constraints of hard chewy confections to a wider existence as flavours, syrupy mixtures poured over desserts or swirled through ice cream, or little chips of sugar, pops of flavour scattered over the top.

3
Spice and Everything Nice

Sugar combines well with many ingredients. Nuts distinguish various species of brittle, a confection with a largely unrecorded past and a vast audience of eager consumers. Brittles are simple confections of nuts or seeds in boiled sugar syrups cooked up to 155°C (310°F). In the USA, peanut brittle-type sweets were already popular in 1912 when Charles Apell gave ten pages of recipes in his *Twentieth Century Candy Teacher*, including delights such as No. 1 Yankee peanut brittle, Spanish peanut squares, hinky-dinky and pecan or walnut brittles. Brittles in the 1950s sold best in autumn and winter, and particularly around Halloween and Thanksgiving.[1] Almond rock and almond hardbake in nineteenth-century England were brittle-type sweets.

In London in 1820, William Jarrin knew almond and sugar mixtures as *nogat* and used them for making ornamental shapes. As *nougatine* (France), *mandorlato* (Italy) and under the catch-all name of *turrón* (Spain), they are popular festive sweets in Mediterranean countries. Eastern examples elide into mixtures that seem toffee-like to British palates. *Sohan* is a traditional Iranian sweet of large, thin, slightly irregular discs of sugar, oil or butter, saffron, honey and almonds, topped with chopped pistachios, 'pure evil, a sticky, greasy, utterly addictive confection that must in part account for the large number of Iranians studying dentistry'.[2] Indians, too, enjoy simple nut and sugar sweets such as *gajjak* – sugar, nuts and sesame seeds. Peanut brittle is also popular in China, as are poppy seed or sesame seed and boiled sugar candies. Sesame sugar was among various types of sugar mentioned in Kuang Tung (Guangdong) around 1700.[3]

Nuts, syrup and beaten egg whites meet in confections known to English speakers as nougat. Starch wafers are frequently used to sandwich the sticky mixture. There are numerous confections which answer this general description: *turrón* (in Spanish), *torrone* (in Italy) and *gaz* or *natif* in Turkey and Iran. Many have regional variations. Pure white, or a warm, cream colour, studded with toasted almonds, pale green pistachios or candied orange peel or apricot paste, they can be scented with honey (now often replaced by glucose syrup) and flower waters, especially in the Islamic world.

Sohan qum, an Iranian sweet of boiled sugar and nuts, whose ingredients and techniques put it somewhere between candied sugar, toffee and brittle.

Artisanal production of nougat: pouring the mixture into a frame to set.

Their textures vary, underpinned by sugar syrup boiled to between 140 and 149°C (284 and 300°F). Lower temperatures make chewy white *nougat de Montelimar*. Higher temperatures caramelize the sugar, giving crunchy textures, more intense flavours and the warm beige-cream colours of Spanish *turrón de Alicante*. For paste-like *turrón de Jijona*, toasted nuts are ground before being added to the mixture. Variable in colour and texture, *torrone* is made all over Italy, from the traditional products of Cremona or Benevento (near Naples, a hazelnut version) to more industrial versions given variety with dried fruit, chocolate or coffee.

In Britain, pale varieties seem to have been popularized at the end of the nineteenth century. An 1890s recipe involves nuts in a cream (fondant) mixture, and around 1900 E. Skuse wrote,

> some very common stuff is vended on barrows, hawked on trays at seaside resorts and sold in small shops chiefly

owned by foreigners in poor neighbourhoods. This latter quality is . . . a mysterious conglomeration of questionable ingredients.[4]

In the USA, nougat soon became a mass-produced confection produced with the aid of mechanized nougat stirrer kettles to lighten heavy work, incorporating industrial ingredients such as fondant, glucose, jelly drops and vegetable fat.

Perhaps the adoption of the name 'nougat' (a French word, from *noix* and *gâteau*, literally nut cake) indicates relative novelty to the English-speaking world. *Torrone* and *turrón* derive from the Latin *torrere*, to toast. *Turrón* has a long history in Spain as a generic term for a range of products, including *turrón de yemas*, more marzipan-like and made with egg yolk, fudge-like walnut *turrón*, hazelnut versions and more recent innovative varieties. Their past is obscure, though they feature in paintings by Juan van der Hamen y León (1596–1631), who worked in Madrid. Their present is obvious, especially at Christmas, when slabs in many shades of cream and brown are displayed in the shops.

The family tree of nougat is multi-branched. Hungarian and Austrian names translate as 'Turkish honey', hinting at the confection's roots and long history in the Islamic world. A tenth-century Persian text describes nougat 'looking as solid and luminous as silver, stuffed with exquisite nuts and flower-like dried fruits, and tasting as soft and sweet as lips'.[5] In Persian culture it is known as *gaz* and packed in fancy wrappers for *Nowrooz* (New Year), a celebration that takes place in early March. In Western industrial confectionery, nougat, or something answering to the name, has been demoted to the status of chocolate-bar filling.

Middle Eastern nougats are sometimes used as an ingredient derived from the roots of some *Gypsophila* species as an alternative to egg whites.[6] As halva root, this is vital in another confection, Turkish *tahin helvası*, a mixture of sugar and tahini (sesame seed paste), also the 'halvah' of Greece and elsewhere in the Middle East. The roots are boiled in water to make a decoction that can be whipped to a white foam. A substance known as saponin is responsible for this, and has sometimes led to the identification of the plant as soapwort, *Saponaria officinalis*.

The foam is mixed with syrup and tahini and beaten and kneaded for a long time. A vivid description of this process survives from nineteenth-century Istanbul. It took three men three hours to beat the mixture; they worked in turn, one taking the beater from another in a fluid, unceasing and constant rhythm until the batch was finished. 'A moment's cessation, an irregularity or a change of movement can compromise the desired result irremediably.'[7] Nineteenth-century halva included mixtures of honey, whole or ground sesame seeds, semolina, nuts and roses producing numerous separate types. In early Turkish texts both egg whites and a

Mixing tahini (beige) and a decoction of *Gypsophila* root beaten with syrup (white) together to make *tahin helvası*, Erdine, Turkey.

Marzipan sweets in fantasy shapes from the Algarve, Portugal, 1990s.

decoction of halva root are cited as possible additions for nougat, suggesting that the pale colour, or the texture produced by these, were distinguishing features.

Marzipan is another pale nutty mixture, a malleable paste of blanched almonds ground and mixed with sugar, rosewater or egg. This is 'a simple thing, which any apothecary can make', wrote Michel de Nostradamus dismissively in 1552.[8] It also has mysterious but probable Islamic roots, a material with many creative possibilities, variable in quality, 'a substance rather than a sweet':

> the English version – bright yellow, cloying, stiff and generally found beneath the icing on fruit cakes. . . . Real marzipan is quite different: a light, moist and deliciously

fresh tasting paste of sugar and almonds (both sweet and bitter), filled with the perfume of the nuts and with the ghost of a crunch of sugar.[9]

Recipes vary in proportions; two parts almonds to one part sugar is considered a good ratio. The best grades are always heated, by addition of hot syrup, mixing over heat or gently baking the finished item.

Sweet almond pastes are found all over Europe, Western Asia and North Africa, linking to a plethora of baked almond confections. A host of these appear as local specialities: Provençal *calissons*, navette-shaped, mixed with candied melon; macaroons, ratafias, *amaretti*, *ricciarelli*, spiced Nurnberg *Lebkuchken*, and perhaps even *alaju*, a soft almond or breadcrumb paste with honey and spices, sandwiched between two large wafers. This, a speciality of parts of eastern and southern Spain, is almost certainly Arabic in origin. Perhaps the mixture of sugar-candy with pine nuts or walnuts of a uniform consistency from which 'some cakes are moulded square, some round and some engraved with figures', described in 1154 in China, is an early mention of a similar confection.[10]

The origin of the name 'marzipan' is unknown. Proposed derivations range from myths about the name of an inventor, and the possibility it comes from the Latin phrase *Marci panis* (St Mark's bread), to elaborate constructions around Arabic words for weights, boxes and caskets. None is entirely convincing. The old English name for the mixture was 'marchpane'.

In sixteenth-century Europe, marzipan was widespread, sometimes as an ingredient, sometimes alone, always delicious. A good modelling medium, it was used in the subtleties displayed between the courses of medieval meals, and in England, in the sixteenth and seventeenth centuries, a marchpane distinguished various celebrations. This was marzipan pressed into a large disc with decoratively crimped edges, iced with sugar and rosewater and decorated with comfits, gilding and moulded fantasy figures of birds, animals and other items. Such discs are still made in Germany, where marzipan is a speciality. It is particularly associated with Lübeck, where the company founded in the early nineteenth century by Johann Georg Niederegger still makes high-quality marzipan confectionery. Marzipan pigs are a Christmas and New Year favourite, bringers of plenty and good luck.

Marzipan shapes are found all over Europe. Some are abstract, such as *figuritas de mazapan de Toledo*, which originated as convent sweets. Sicilian *frutti di Martorana*, originally another convent speciality, are gaudily painted marzipan fruit or vegetables. Ottoman Turkey used such items too, glazed with a gum tragacanth solution and sugar syrup, and the French make numerous shapes – fruits, vegetables, seafood and other fantasies – from marzipan. Very elaborate versions were produced by skilled confectioners in the past. A recipe from 1820 described how to mould sugar paste around an almond to make a peach 'stone'; almond paste was moulded round this to shape the fruit itself, and the whole dipped in isinglass jelly, giving the slightly yielding surface of ripeness. A light dusting of starch imitated a just-harvested bloom.

Sugar-covered spices or nuts are another category of sweets, important markers of festivity in the Middle East and Europe. Once known as comfits and also as sugar-plums, these have lost their collective identity in the Anglophone world, although individually – sugared almonds, aniseed balls, Good & Plenty, jelly beans, M&Ms, Smarties, mint imperials, sprinkles – they remain favourites. Confectioners classify them under the prosaic collectives of panned sweets or pan work (the process for making them is called panning), or use the French term *dragées*.

Box with *frutti di Martorana*, shaped and painted marzipan, Sicily.

Panning is an ancient technique, perhaps with honey-based precursors in classical Europe. The method is also widespread across southwest and central Asia. Whatever their origins, such confections were known in the Middle Ages, initially imported from the East, then later made by European apothecaries. Sugar and the various seeds and other centres had medicinal applications, and panning is still used pharmaceutically to sugar-coat drugs.

The word 'comfit' shares its origin with 'confection' and has parallels in other languages, notably Italian, as *confetto* (plural *confetti*), originally meaning a small sweet. Decorative

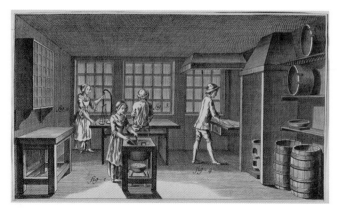

Jean le Rond d'Alembert and Denis Diderot (after), *Confectioner's Shop: Process of Smoothing Sugar-plums* (comfits), mid-18th century, etching.

and abundant, they came to denote celebration, distributed at formal meals and festivities. Comfits also had a central role in late medieval households as an aid to digestion (rather as after-dinner mints are now eaten).

Manufacture is simple in outline, building up thin layers of sugar on the surface of spices, nuts, little pieces of fruit or sugar paste, jelly, chocolate or candied fruit. In pre-industrial times, items for centres, for instance, caraway seeds, enormously popular in Britain throughout the early modern period, were placed in a balancing pan,

> a large copper pan suspended from the ceiling or beam
> by means of two chains attached to a bar with a hook
> and swivel in the centre . . . to be kept at a moderate heat
> . . . and swung backwards or forwards.[11]

The seeds were stirred, warmed and dried in this, then just enough syrup was added to wet them. Syrups used here were at the low end of the boiling scale, just a few degrees above

100°C (212°F). After each charge of syrup the confectioner shook the pan to keep the sweets in motion, stirring and rubbing them. The water evaporated, leaving a thin opaque coat of sugar. Many repetitions, a process known as engrossing, produced ever larger comfits. Although this sounds simple, to make comfits consistently well requires skill. After several charges, they must be dried, or the coating develops a greyish cast. A degree or two in syrup temperature produces the difference between a beautiful smooth surface (*perlée* in French) and a knobbly, 'ragged' or *lisée* one.

The seventeenth-century polymath Sir Hugh Platt provided an exceptional description of comfit making. He notes items used for centres: aniseed, coriander seeds, caraway, fennel, lengths of cinnamon, orange rind, a spiced bread paste and powdered sugar itself. Different colours were produced by adding dyes to the syrup, and surface textures varied. For centuries, a distinction was made between small and large comfits, as the latter required more sugar, a consideration when it was expensive.

The French became masters of comfit making. As early as the thirteenth century Verdun was mentioned in this context. Metz, Nancy, Toulouse and Paris were also associated with comfits, and Flavigny (in Burgundy) developed anise comfits as a convent speciality. The notion of comfits was taken by the Portuguese to Japan, where little round sugar sweets with an irregular surface are still known as *konpeitō*, 'a small toffee sphere . . . with a pimply surface, made from sugar, water, and flour, in a variety of colours'.[12] The name derives from Portuguese *confeito*, and these too originally had a seed, sesame or poppy, in the middle.

Variety in hard comfits is a matter of shape, colour and finish. Pebble-like, shapes echo items used in the centres – round for coriander, oval for caraway, egg-shapes for almonds, long slender shapes for the cinnamon stick 'long' comfits of historic practice. The inhabitants of early modern Europe seem to have been fascinated by ragged comfits, favourite subjects in still-life paintings. Rough or knobbly comfits lost their attraction in the Western world but survive where craft confectioners still work, for instance as Afghan *noql*, sugared almonds with a bobbled surface of numerous small accretions of sugar.

White is the default colour, and red (from plant pigments or cochineal) its usual counterpoise in the early modern period. Saffron (yellow) and spinach (green) were also used. More intense colour came from mineral-derived pigments, which confectioners knew were toxic, but were not always scrupulous about avoiding. In the mid-nineteenth century new brilliantly coloured dyes from coal tar were exploited to the full, giving the rainbow-coloured forms of comfits now known. The tiniest variety are nonpareils, better known to English speakers as hundreds and thousands, or sprinkles. These use sugar crystals as centres and allow confectioners to play with colour. To the mystification of generations of children, these tiny sweets, often scattered over cakes and desserts, display a range of colours – each colour batch individually panned and all mixed together afterwards. Such sweets are also the nuclei of the largest comfits, the giant penny candies known in Britain as gobstoppers and North America as jaw-breakers. These are a particular object of fascination, changing colour as they become smaller, needing frequent inspection and comparison by their young consumers. This magical effect originated in the confectioners' habit of using scrap syrup from other processes, giving randomly coloured layers.

Cheap sugar and mechanization affected comfit production in the nineteenth century. A new mechanical pan was introduced in Paris in the mid-century, in the shape of a ball or orange, about one-third cut off; inside there is a lining, between which and the outside through its whole interior the steam passes. Some are made to revolve vertically on an axis, others to oscillate on another principle.[13]

Steam regulated the heat and drove the pans. A system of pipes extracted dust and water vapour. The tedious process of alternate panning and drying – with each skilled confectioner making a daily maximum of about 23 kg of finished sweets – became an industrial one and by the end of the nineteenth century a skilled workman could superintend 'nearly a dozen steam pans, which would produce three or four tons a week', in a process cleaner and less risky than the old one done by fire heat.[14]

Panned goods have always been a special branch of confectionery. Many twentieth-century confectionery factories

Revolving steam pans for making dragées, Verdun, France, 1926.

did not have a panned goods department, but some made them exclusively. Traditional comfits, such as nut-based ones – almonds, pistachios, pine nuts – still flourish, and, in North America, sugar-coated peanuts are an essential element of M&Ms. Nonpareils are scattered over chocolate drops, a confection made since the eighteenth century, and shiny silver dragées decorate cakes.

Spiced comfits are still available. Smooth, pale anise flavoured comfits are made in France; the British equivalent are the more violently flavoured and red-coloured aniseed balls. Liquorice torpedoes (Britain) and Good & Plenty (a North

Jelly Belly Original Gourmet Jelly Beans on sale from dispensers in the USA, 2016.

American brand originating in the late nineteenth century) echo the long comfit tradition. The intense cinnamon flavour of Atomic Fireballs issues a challenge to North American children. The main descendants, though, in spirit if not entirely in form, are probably TicTacs, made 'by a unique spinning technology to enrobe the mint at the heart of each sweet with hundreds of fine layers of vanilla coating',[15] devised by the Italian company Ferrero in 1969, ubiquitous and abundant, in exactly the same way as the comfits of old.

Panning in Europe and North America also developed a new direction in the twentieth century. Confectioners discovered that the size, shape, interior finish of the pan and speed at which it rotated allowed the creation of different products. Using glucose syrup, soft-textured comfit varieties became possible. These were built up around pieces of soft sugar paste or tiny spheres of jelly, made in small-diameter, swiftly rotating pans.

Jelly beans, a North American favourite, were in production by the first decade of the twentieth century, their centres made by starch moulding. A popular penny candy, in the last few decades they have received a boost, partly because U.S. President Ronald Reagan claimed they were his favourite candy, and partly by the development of the Jelly Belly brand – small, brilliantly coloured and brilliantly marketed. In the twenty-first century, confectionery imitated literature as Bertie Bott's Every Flavour Beans went into production, riding on the success of the *Harry Potter* series.

Chocolate was part of this new generation of comfits, panned with thin, crisp sugar shells and a final coating of brilliant colour. In the UK, the Rowntree company produced these in 1882 as chocolate beans; rebranded in 1937 as Smarties, they have been popular ever since. North Americans grow up with M&Ms, the 'Ms' standing for Forrest E. Mars and Bruce

Murrie, son of the president of the Hershey company. These, Joël Glenn Brenner remarked, were 'born out of war, made specifically for the soldiers of WWII who were stationed in tropical climates where chocolate bars would melt'.[16]

Another vast and widespread group of confections is based on sugar and fruit. Across the world, locally grown items provide the basis for myriad preserves, pastes, jellies, jams and candied fruit. Pleasant luxuries, they emerged from a desire to store summer abundance for winter and enhance any medicinal qualities the fruit was considered to possess. They exist in all major culinary cultures of the world, having evolved in the distant past (in Eurasia) or under European influence elsewhere. Variety is provided by the fruit, flowers or vegetables that are important in the culture concerned.

Historically, fruit preserving was important in the work of the confectioner. Marmalades, jams and jellies of European and North American practice originated in a preserve of quinces stored in honey or *defrutum* (boiled grape must). From this developed fruit and sugar pastes, eventually giving rise to the citrus preserves of the British breakfast table. Of the original quince type, almost every country round the Mediterranean has its own version: *marmelata* (Portugal), *membrillo* (Spain), *seferjal* (Arabic). Quinces, relatively easy to store, made preserves of a glorious red, 'like an oriental ruby', according to Michel de Nostradamus. This description could still apply to *cotignac d'Orléans*, a traditional confection of Orléans in France, poured into tiny woodchip boxes, or moulded in larger discs.

Syrup-preserved fruit recipes occupy much space in historic texts, but canning and freezing removed the need for these. Artisan confectioners concentrate on fruit pastes, jellies and candied fruit, although 'spoon sweets' have long been an important hospitality ritual in some eastern Mediterranean

Blocks of deep red *goiabada,* guava paste, for sale on a street stall, Minas Gerais, Brazil. In this tropical setting, guavas substitute for the quinces traditionally used in Portugal.

countries. As court confectioner Friedrich Unger observed in the 1830s,

> Not only in Greece but also in European Turkey and apparently throughout the Orient it is customary that the housewife offer every guest preserves or *scherbet,* of which a spoonful is taken, followed by a drink of water and then a pipe and coffee.[17]

It is a ritual that survives, though possibly with less emphasis on pipes of tobacco.

The finest preserves are whole candied fruits, made by steeping gently cooked fruit in sugar syrup. Over a period

OVERLEAF: A vast selection of dried and candied fruit displayed for sale in Germany, 2014.

of days the concentration of sugar in the syrup is gradually increased so that, as osmosis draws water out of the cells of the fruit, sugar gradually replaces it. Fully candied fruit can be stored in syrup, a confection formerly known as *succade* or *suckets* in English, or removed and dried (not to be confused with fruit dried without sugar, purely by desiccation). It has been a luxury food for centuries. In the 1950s, Elizabeth David said,

> Italian preserved and candied fruit is spectacular. Whole pineapples, melons, citrons, oranges, figs, apricots, red and green plums, pears, even bananas in their skins, are sugared in the most skillful way, and make marvellous displays in the shops of Genoa and Milan.[18]

A much wider range of items were candied in the past. *Marrons glacées* are still a French speciality; so is intense green angelica, which recalls a habit of candying lettuce or mallow stems as medicinal confections, as does ginger root preserved in syrup. Ginger travelled far; it is native to Indo-China. In the Middle Ages, apothecaries knew three types – Colombine, Valadine and Maikine, names that denoted associations with places such as Quilon (Kollam on the west coast of India) and Mecca – and made preserves from them all.

Flower petals, too, made preserves, valued for their perfumes. Roses, violets and orange flowers were all cooked in sugar, the result sometimes known as pralines. Alternatively, they could be candied, suspended in warm syrup. Borage, pot marigolds and other flowers were candied for colour, flavour or medicine. Candied rose or violets are still specialities of a few artisan confectioners in countries such as France, Spain and further afield. Turkish *gülbseker* is a preserve of sugar and rose petals.

The traditions of Asia still use a variety of plant materials. Preserves of watermelon peel, of aubergines or sour cherries are Middle Eastern specialities. Candied gourd or pumpkin, *kumrar mithai*, is a south Asian favourite. In *Bengal Sweets*, Mrs Haldar gave instructions on how to make this using the flesh of white pumpkins. Cut in small cubes, soaked in water, boiled in alum solution, drained and washed, they are boiled in syrup until tender, and perfumed with rose otto. If dried, they kept for a long time. Soaking in limewater or alum helps to develop an extraordinary succulent texture and glass-like transparency, as well as removing bitterness. A pleasant treat, she says, they 'are easily prescribed to convalescents', echoing Michel de Nostradamus four centuries earlier, who mentioned in his recipe that 'these preserved pumpkins are very good to eat

Bowls of candied fruit and seeds in Vietnam, celebratory foods for Tết, the lunar New Year.

. . . they are also useful as a cooling medicine . . . to alleviate too much heat of the heart and liver.'[19]

Preserved fruit is a branch of confectionery that has long been a favourite in China (though 'Chinese figs', popular in Britain in the twentieth century, were jellied sweets with no discernible Chinese connections). Sugar-preserved oranges were recorded in China in the thirteenth century, and candied fruit was exported from China to the Spanish in the Philippines in the seventeenth century. In the 1840s, Montgomery Martin, an English visitor, noted that 'the Chinese candy almost everything eatable, such as millet seeds, bamboo shoots, ginger, etc., which are hawked about the streets and exported to all countries, particularly to India, the United States and South America.'[20] His list included winter melons, watermelons, oranges, tangerines, kumquats and plums. Many sugar-preserved items are still made: the author bought candied plums, osmanthus fruit (*Osmanthus fragrans*), lotus root, melon or gourd, and little pieces of candied lemon or orange peel in Hong Kong in the 1990s. It is difficult to imagine some truly Eastern fruity sweets, such as durian-flavoured candy, a product of the modern Southeast Asian confectionery industry, becoming popular in the English-speaking world (durian has a notoriously odd, and, to those unaccustomed to it, disagreeable odour).

In the Philippines, native tradition, Chinese influence, four centuries of Spanish colonization and fifty years of American political dominance have given ample scope for the development of confectionery. Under this influence, sugary pastes based on fruit or *ube* (purple yam) developed, and larger fruits were preserved in syrup by candying. Until recently, the peel of citrus fruit was sometimes carved in elaborate patterns, a device once fashionable in seventeenth-century Europe. Sugar-preserved fruit and fruit pastes are also an important element of Latin American confectionery, especially in Mexico. The Japanese candy beans and use a sweetened paste made from adzuki beans as a filling for various sweet confections such as *mochi*, a type of rice paste dumpling, or *monaka*, wafer shells, to make uniquely Japanese confections.

Milk is the basis for many important confectionery traditions. As *dulce de leche*, one of these belongs to Central and South America. A simple way of making this is to cook a tin of sweetened condensed milk in boiling water for several hours, although in earlier times the milk must have been boiled in an open pan. Eventually it becomes a mid-brown semi-solid and the naturally occurring milk sugar, lactose, plus any added sugar, gives a caramelized flavour. Used both as a confection and an ingredient in other items, such as cakes and creams, it has many names: '*cajeta* in Mexico (from the small wooden boxes in which it was traditionally sold), *manjar* ("delicacy") in Peru and Chile, *doce de liete* in Brazil, and *arequipe* in Colombia'.[21] Prolonged boiling produces fudgy versions; among these Mexican varieties include *jamoncillo* and Glorias, the latter a trade name for large candies resembling sticky fudge, made from goat's milk and chopped pecans.

In the Philippines, *pastillas de leche* are sweets based on reduced milk. Unlike their Latin American counterparts, they are small, neat pale cylinders rolled in fine sugar. These are remarkable not just for delectable flavour and texture, but for their traditional decorative wrappers:

> the centerpiece of a fiesta table is always a three-tiered epergne filled with pastillas de leche, all of them wrapped in papel de japon of different colours, cut out in designs of flowers, leaves, birds, butterflies . . . These lacey tails float down from the dish . . . proclaiming both sweetness and beauty.[22]

Mexican favourites Glorias, sticky candies made of *dulche de leche*.

The origins of all these condensed milk sweets, like those of fudge, are unknown. The common history of Spanish colonization in South America and the Philippines suggests Iberian precursors, but no obvious ancestor for them has been detected in Spanish literature or culture.

The Indian subcontinent has a major tradition of milk, derived from cattle and therefore sacred, in confections. The milk product ghee is especially important in Hindu religious beliefs and India's highly stratified traditional social system. It renders any foodstuff produced by a member of a lower caste 'pure' and acceptable to members of higher castes. Sometime in the first millennium BC both the sacred aspect of milk products and the knowledge of sugar production and processing developed on the Indian subcontinent, but the story is a tangled web of myth, fable and history. Indian texts had a fluid development, and the terms for sweet foods and forms of sugar found in them have no agreed definitions.

Categorizing Indian sweets is a futile exercise. Indian landscapes and food cultures vary widely, and confections lie on a continuum with other foods, rather than being seen as extra to the diet, as they tend to be in the Western world. 'Some are variants of those found over an area extending from Turkey through the Middle East, and Central Asia to India. . . . Universally popular sweets include barfi, laddus, jalebi, halvah.'[23] Others are restricted to one town or small area.

What is certain is that combinations of milk and honey or sugar have been used for sweet foods for thousands of years. The 'treasures of milk', as writer on Indian cookery Yamuna Devi called them, include ghee (clarified butter), *khoa* (condensed milk) and *chhena*, or *chhana* (fresh cheese curd). Ghee and *khoa* are used across the region for flavour and texture. Milk is stirred constantly in open pans, reducing to a half, a third, a sixth or an eighth of the original volume, each stage with a specific use. *Khoa* is an eighth, the most reduced, a paste-like substance with a sweet, caramelized undertone, which sets when cold, the basis of distinctive milk confections.[24] When

Filipino *pastillas de leche* with the traditional cut paper wrappers used for celebrations.

cold, it is pulverized and sifted for use. Commercially produced dried milk is sometimes substituted, especially in domestic situations.

Khoa is most important in confections known collectively as *barfi*, borrowed from a word meaning 'ice' in Persian. The sugar, reduced milk flavours and textures make *barfi* reminiscent of fudge to Westerners, but it is paler in colour. There are many varieties, flavoured with pistachios, almonds, cashews or gram (chickpea) flour. Perhaps the biggest change for this sweet in centuries is convenience:

> *Barfi* has changed very little since its beginnings, but with the twentieth century came powdered milk . . . Rather than boiling the milk to make a paste, modern cooks can stir powdered milk into a flavoured syrup and cook it very briefly until thick.[25]

Khoa also goes into *raskara*, a coconut-based confection from southern and eastern India. Exotic flavour notes of black pepper and camphor stop this seeming too much like coconut ice. *Pera* or *peda* are balls or discs of *khoa* and sugar often stamped with a flower motif. Found in many parts of the country, they are important as offerings for the goddess Kali in Kolkata.

In modern practice, confections cover a wide range of items, including soft, creamy-textured dishes and *kulfi* (ice cream). Others are deep-fried and dropped into cold syrup afterwards, processes certainly not associated with European or North American candies. The best-known items produced this way are *gulab jamun*, made from a paste of reduced milk and flour, and *jalebi*, squiggles of batter containing *besan* (chickpea flour). Mysore *pak*, a famous South Indian sweet, is made by adding toasted besan to a buttery syrup and stirring until it froths, producing a hard, crumbly texture when cool. *Laddu*, one of the principal confections of Indian food, based on ghee, besan and sugar, may have innumerable minor variations according to maker and place, but are essentially the same everywhere, used rather in the way that cake is in Britain, as an all-purpose snack or celebration food.

Halva, too, has limited archetypes in the Indian subcontinent – semolina based, like fluffy puddings, or vegetable halvas (carrot, winter melon, yam or summer squash) cooked in cream and reduced to a paste-like fudge. Good-quality ghee is essential for good halva. The sweetmeat is important in northern India and into Bengal, where semolina and chickpea halva is known as *mohanbhog*, 'a captivating dish'. Ingredients alien to Western confectionery are used: for mung dahl halva, the soaked raw dahl is ground, fried in ghee to kill the 'raw' smell, cooked with milk, sugar and khoa, and finished off with chopped almonds and pistachios; 'a few crimson rose petals will lend the dish additional grace.'[26] In Pakistan, one type of halva is associated with Karachi, rubbery in texture, translucent, randomly scattered with nuts and coloured in brilliant shades of orange, green, yellow and reds, a little like a vivid Day-Glo version of Turkish delight.

The hard or semi-hard confections, various types of halva or *barfi* – slabs, wedges, lozenges of many-coloured pastes, sugar-glazed rings, flower-stamped discs or simple spheres, often enhanced with sheets of *vark*, silver leaf – are stacked in sweetshop windows or displayed on street stalls. Such shops are now also to be found in British cities wherever there is a significant population from the Indian subcontinent; Ambala Foods, one of the best-known Indian sweet companies, was founded in 1964.

Chhana, made by curdling and straining fresh milk, closely identified with Bengali practice, is unique in confectionery traditions. Confectioners curdle hot milk with lime juice, citric acid or whey, and strain out the solid portion. Curdling is called 'cutting' or 'tearing' the milk. For a long time this was considered a sin, and opinion varies over how this technique arose. One possibility is Portuguese influence in the seventeenth century, with the use of *chhana* as a major ingredient in sweetmeats emerging in the mid-nineteenth century.[27]

Chhana is important for both soft, syrup-soaked sweets, more like desserts to Westerners, and for *sandesh*. This, sometimes called 'the Queen of Bengal sweets', comes in so many varieties 'that it is not possible to give a comprehensive list'.[28] *Sandesh* has a short shelf life, between a few hours and a couple of days, but in other respects – size, use, a fantasy element in shapes, names and flavours – it fulfils attributes of candy or sweets as used in the Western world, evolving subject to fashion with makers embroidering on old themes. The basis is essentially the same; it is the form that differs.

Shop window display, Goa, India, including several types of *barfi* (top row); *kumrar mithai*, preserved pumpkin (centre left); and *laddu* decorated with vark, silver leaf (centre).

A group of ceramic moulds for *sandesh*, each between 2 and 3 cm in length, from Kalighat, Kolkata.

Made by mixing *chhana* with sugar in varying proportions, *sandesh* has subtle flavours and textures. The best involves a high proportion of soft *chhana*, mixed with dry sugar and cooked over a low heat until it draws away from the side of the pan. Flavourings listed in the early twentieth century included lemon zest, musk, cardamom, pistachios, poppy seed, saffron, rose, nuts and, a novelty in Indian sweets at that time, cocoa powder. Newly produced *gur* (a winter product in Bengal) is a prized flavour:

> The arrival of gur in the market is the signal for the professional sweet-makers to start preparing one of their most popular products, sandesh flavoured with the new gur. This nalen gurer sandesh has a browny-pink tinge and is very dear to the plump Bengali's heart.[29]

Decorative moulds are used for *sandesh*, made from wood or ceramics in the shape of rosettes, wheels, fruits and fish.

Sandesh, a favourite Bengali confection, shaped in a traditional round ceramic mould and presented on a clay cup.

Names include descriptions of shape, feelings associated with consuming *sandesh*, analogies derived from comparisons with fruits, and abstract ideas of blessings and good wishes. The influence of the British Raj showed in the past in names such as 'God Save the King' and 'Forget-me-not'.

In the 'everything nice' lexicon of confectionery, another unique confectionery tradition, this time based on egg yolks, comes from Iberian cultures and areas influenced by them. These pop up in unlikely places, such as Thailand, possibly originating from Portuguese traditions. Vividly golden in colour, richly eggy in taste, with curious and distinctive textures, making them is a gentle process, as the proteins in egg yolk coagulate at about 70°C (158°F). Spanish *yemas* (literally, yolks) and Portuguese *ovos moles* (soft eggs) both combine egg yolks and sugar, cooked together to a semi-solid texture. In Spain the most famous are possibly *yemas de Santa Teresa de Avila*, named for the saint and the city with which she is associated. Gently cooked with cinnamon-flavoured syrup, the mix is allowed to cool, rolled into little yolk-sized balls, dusted with sugar and presented in paper cases. *Yemas* of this general type are also made in the Philippines, modern versions being made with condensed milk. *Ovos moles* are made by a similar process but are more liquid. They are a speciality of the town of Aveiro in northern Portugal, and are used to fill special fragile papery white wafer cases made in the shape of seashells. The custardy substance is also used as an element of many other cakes and pastries, both in Portugal and Brazil (Northern Europeans might also think of Dutch Advocaat liqueur).

Egg yolks and syrup have other creative possibilities. *Fios de ovos*, 'egg threads', are made by drizzling beaten yolk through a special container into boiling syrup. Popular in Portugal and Brazil, Portuguese influence almost certainly took these elsewhere, to Japan as *keiran somen* and Thailand as *foi thong*, 'golden strands'. (*Abryshum kebab*, apparently entirely unconnected with Iberian influence, made in parts of central Asia,

Making *thong yod*, a Thai confection made from drops of beaten egg yolk cooked in boiling syrup.

consists of threads of egg fried in oil before submersion in cardamom-flavoured syrup.)

Sheets of egg yolk cooked on top of hot syrup make *trouxas de ovos* in Portugal, often rolled into cylinders, filled with a portion of *fios de ovos*, and glazed with more syrup. *Trouxas de ovos* may be the origin of Thai *thong yip*, produced in an identical fashion and formed into little star or flower shapes, 'whose golden colour symbolizes victory and wealth . . . whose sugary taste promises sweetness and happiness'.[30]

These eggy confections were possibly convent specialities, exported around the early modern world with Catholicism. Egg whites have uses in other sweets, including marzipan, nougats, meringues and almond-based pastes and macaroons, or they may have been used in clearing wine at the end of fermentation. In the Philippines, a 'unique local custom' used the whites in mortar for large buildings, such as churches built by European colonizers.[31] An acquired taste, the origins of these sweets remains a mystery, but one aspect – their glorious golden yellow colour – must always have been valued.

4
Some Oddities

Among the bewildering variety of North American and European confections are some that seem distinctly odd: perfumed, fizzy, sour, elastic in texture, black or dark red, or made to be chewed and then discarded. Based on sugar paste, sherbet, liquorice, marshmallow, fruit gums and chewing gum, they have distinct histories illuminating relationships with medicines and drinks. Disparate in form, they all use binders, including gums, pectin, gelatine or starch, to give texture and structure and to form outlandish fantasies.

Sugar paste, like marzipan, is really a substance, not a sweet, used both as a decorative medium and to make small items. From the sixteenth century and probably long before confectioners made it from powdered sugar mixed with soaked gum arabic or gum tragacanth, perfumed with spices, rosewater or musk. Fresh, it is like clay; dry, it becomes delicate and fragile. Inedible versions, mixed with starch or plaster, were made purely for decorative use, coloured, painted and gilded.

In post-medieval Europe sugar paste was highly valued for whiteness and lightness, unusual attributes in the early modern world where porcelain was rare and ceramics tended to be heavy and robust. Together with silver, gold, fine glass

Arnold van Westerhout after Giovanni Battista Lenardi, *Trionfi or Sugar Sculptures of Cybele and Juno*, c. 1687, etching.

and linen, sugar paste was a precious decorative material. It was especially important in Italy for making *trionfi di tavola*, elaborate and highly accomplished sculptures designed to entertain and flatter the nobility. A remarkable example was recorded in Venice in 1574, where a *collazione* was given for Henri III of France. At this, 'a legion of sugar-paste popes, kings, cardinals, doges, gods, and beasts of every description stood guard over a feast of sweetmeats . . . there were apparently three hundred of these figures gilded with silver and gold'.[1]

To make *trionfi di tavola* demanded skill, and some figures were designed by Jacopo Sansovino, sculptor and architect. They were part of increasingly elaborate entertainments, which included tables that turned into fountains and sideboards that rose out of the floor, covered in plates, cups and napkins, all made out of sugar paste, contrived for royalty.[2] Descriptions of these banquets spread and wealthy Europeans all wanted sugar paste on their tables. Details of how to make it and shape it into delicate plates, bowls and drinking vessels were given in sixteenth-century books of 'secrets' such as that by Alexis of Piedmont. There were smaller novelties as well. Walnut shells were made out of brown paste pressed in moulds; each was filled with little comfits and a tiny scroll of paper inscribed with lines of poetry. Little cachous cut from musk- and ambergris-perfumed paste sweetened the breath of those with sugar-rotted teeth.

Trionfi inspired decorative sugarwork that embellished fashionable tables over the next four centuries. Eighteenth-century desserts featured large mirrored plateaux set in the middle of the table covered with parterres, elaborate representations of formal gardens entirely made of sugar. The paths were coloured sugar sand, small comfits represented pebbles, rock candy made sparkling highlights and paste was shaped into fruit, flowers, rocky islands, buildings and decorative figures to further ornament these. These, fragile models of gods, goddesses and people of all stations of life, influenced

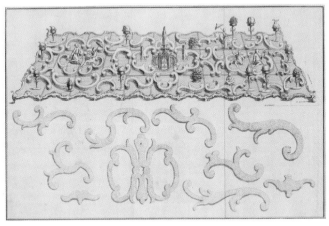

Anon., plate from Joseph Gilliers, *Le Cannemeliste français* (1751), etching. This depicts a layout for a sugar parterre, a fashionable 18th-century table decoration made from various materials including sugar paste, cast sugar, comfits and coloured sugar crystals.

the products of European ceramics manufacturers, and when they discovered how to make porcelain in the eighteenth century, their designs and techniques drew on centuries of accumulated sugarworking skill.

Architectural displays for the dining table were revived in the early nineteenth century, especially by the fashionable chef and confectioner Antonin Carême in Europe, and flourished on the western side of the Atlantic at events such as presidential parties. Not until the First World War, when the taste for grandeur was lost, along with the finance and skills, did the fashion really diminish. Paste is now bought ready-made, glycerine, corn starch or vegetable shortening added for easier working. *Pastillage* is a form of paste that sets hard, used for strength, definition and durability. It is still subject to fashions. In the late twentieth century it was a favoured medium for decorating celebration cakes, draped to cover them, pierced, frilled, pressed into moulds or modelled freehand according to skill and fancy, especially as flowers.

Sugar paste also made lozenges for delivering drugs, an important and enduring use overtly linked to the confectioner-apothecary. A known quantity of drug was mixed with a specific amount of paste. Carefully rolled and divided, each portion contained a measured dose. This was a specialist trade that required constant practice for good results. Lozenge-making industrialized in the mid-nineteenth century when J. W. Pepper took out a u.s. patent. His machinery, which mixed, rolled and stamped the paste, meant that only a superintendent was required to turn out a high volume of lozenges daily.

Compression developed as an alternative means of holding sugar and flavour together, punching out discs and circles under high pressure. Wholly a product of the industrial confectioner, these require various binders and lubricants,

Higashi, Japanese confections for the tea ceremony, made by pressing a mixture of rice flour and fine sugar into wooden moulds.

and nuances such as dextrose monohydrate, a specific form of glucose, preferred because the form its crystals take aids cohesion. Some very well-known candies are made by compression: mint-flavoured Lifesavers, invented in 1912 by Clarence Crane in Cleveland, Ohio, and Polo mints, devised by Rowntree's in the UK in 1948, are made this way. Alongside these, softer 'cream' pastes, which form the fillings for Liquorice Allsorts, also developed; they contain fat and glycerine.

Higashi, made in Japan, might be counted as a form of compressed candy, albeit a traditional confection with a very different background. The finest use a special type of sugar known as *wasanbon*, harvested from *Saccharum sinense*, Chinese sugar cane. Refined by a complex process, the juice, after boiling to form a raw brown sugar, is wrapped in a cloth and pressed, then kneaded with water to remove the molasses. Repeated three times, the process is followed by a week's drying. This produces an 'extremely fine sugar that has a very important place in the making of top-quality *higashi*'.[5]

Mixed with rice flour and coloured, the sugar is pressed into decorative moulds. *Higashi* look beautiful, gorgeously shaped and coloured, often according to the season, but to Westerners who try them, they taste of raw rice powder and sweetness. Their primary role is as part of the tea ceremony, when each participant takes one to sweeten the mouth before drinking bitter powdered green tea.

Back in Britain, conversation lozenges, made of sugar paste with words or sentences stamped on them, originated as a nineteenth-century fad. Another development of this period was powder mixes of bicarbonate of soda, citric or tartaric acid and sugar for effervescent lemonade or sherbet beverages. The confectioner's skills as producer of drinks and ices were the source of this novelty. It was a shortcut based on the older *sharbat*, flavoured syrups, diluted with water and chilled to make refreshing drinks in Turkey, Persia and Arab-influenced countries, which had become fashionable

Lokhusa şerbeti, lozenges of cinnamon-flavoured sugar scattered with pine nut comfits, on display in a confectioner's window, Istanbul, 2012.

in Europe as well. In Turkey, syrups, flavoured pastes or solid tablets of sugar for these survive, still made by professional confectioners, such as *lohusa şerbeti* for 'hot spiced sherbet traditionally made after the birth of a child to give the new mother energy and improve her supply of milk'.[4] Mostly they are squeezed off the shelves by bottled fizzy drinks – themselves, ironically, developments of the effervescent lemonade that English sherbet imitated.

Powdered sherbet mixes were adopted as cheap sweets by children. Compressed tablets combined with sherbet and the idea of conversation lozenges to produce Love Hearts, an iconic sweet of British childhoods. The powder became a filling for sherbet lemons, boiled sugar sweets, or was packed in an envelope with a boiled sugar lolly for dipping, or in paper cylinders with a liquorice tube to suck it through. In North America sherbet developed into ices, and in continental Europe it became sorbet, water ice. In Britain, sorbet is also an elegant palate refresher, but sherbet marches on, a childhood triviality.

Liquorice, another iconic sweet of childhood, is made from an extract of the roots of *Glycyrrhiza glabra*, native to the Mediterranean and parts of Asia. Extremely sweet, the dried roots were once essential to every medicine chest. Liquorice has therapeutic effects on coughs and colds, making it a true confection, and it is the extract, condensed to 'block juice', a shiny tar-like solid, that is used. Sweets made from it are a rite of passage in Western European countries, America and the Antipodes. Darkest black, semi-translucent brown or a rich dark red, depending on place, the earthy flavour is partially masked by other essences; aniseed is a favourite. A salty note is added in some countries, giving a very strange flavour to those not accustomed to it. Popular in Scandinavian countries, this is called *salmiak* (derived from *sal ammoniac*, ammonium chloride), the ingredient that gives this unique taste. The Dutch, too, are enthusiastic consumers of this type of liquorice, which they call *drop*:

> Holland . . . is liquorice-land. There are literally dozens of kinds, in all shapes and sizes, in varying degrees of hardness, sweetness and saltiness, and added extras like bay leaf and honey are enjoyed as long as there is not too much adulteration of the pure liquorice flavour. Liquorice Allsorts, known here as *Englese drop* or English liquorice, are waved aside indulgently as lightweights.[5]

The variously hard, chewy or elastic textures of liquorice confections are derived from ingredients that bind and give shape to sugar, liquorice extract and flavourings. Wheat flour gives a stretchy, resilient quality to British liquorice, and gum gives structure to the fantasy shapes of a drop. The gothic blackness of liquorice makes buttons or coins with impressed patterns, as in Pontefract Cakes (a traditional English form), sinister black cats, jolly farm or circus animals, plain lozenges or snake-like spirals, a contrast to the usual palette of confectionery colours.

Medicinal uses of liquorice are recalled by various tiny liquorice sweets – French brands Cachou Lajaunie (originally breath fresheners) in tiny yellow tins and Zan (now owned by Haribo), Amarelli (originating in 1731) in Italy and, in Britain, powerfully flavoured Fisherman's Friends, Tics or Imps. The major British brand is Bassett's, whose Liquorice Allsorts are surely influenced by Modernist art, blocks of graphic black of liquorice sandwiched with white or brightly coloured soft sugar paste, mixed with short cylinders of plain black liquorice and a liberal addition of 'spogs' – aniseedy gum discs covered in tiny blue or pink comfits.

Marshmallow is exactly the reverse of liquorice: pale, pastel, pillowy, sweetness and light. This belies its origins, based on the sap of *Althaea officinalis*, which made a heavy, bitter paste, soothing for coughs and sore throats. Apple jelly replaced the original plant; later, egg whites lightened the mix. A type of candy similar to this is still made in Russia as *pastila*. Traditional French *pâte de guimauve*, closer to modern marshmallow and now usually foamed with gelatine, has a slightly tough texture.

Light-as-air marshmallows foamed with gelatine were 'a rare favourite in the United States', said an English confectioner in the early twentieth century.[6] A special marshmallow kettle with a beater, steam-heated, foamed the mixture and lightened the load for makers, and starch moulding shaped marshmallow bananas and marshmallow 'penny goods'. Industrialization advanced in 1954 with an extrusion process that forced the mix through a chute, simultaneously cutting it to size. The inventor of this was Alex Doumakes, of the USA company Doumak. Marshmallow became an ingredient in mallowmars, moonpies and, in the UK, 'teacakes' (cookies topped with marshmallow and coated with chocolate); it also went into home-made rocky road, the iconic s'mores of campfire cookery and marshmallow fluff to spread in sandwiches.

The foamed mixes of the modern confectionery line are shaped in whatever forms catch the imagination: rabbits, flowers, shrimps, toadstools, front teeth, strawberries, twisted cables, mice. In the USA, Peeps have become a cult favourite – decorative shapes in zingy colours, overtly frivolous.

Fruit jellies and gums are derived from the preserving tradition. Gelling agents are vital in these. Elegant French *confiseries* still display expensive and luxurious *pâtes de fruits* in jewel colours – yellow, orange, reds and rich, dark purples – but fruit-based confections also escaped artisan constraints in the nineteenth century. A British fad for jujubes, named for Chinese dates or jujubes (actually the fruit of a plant of the buckthorn family), was apparent by 1830 when William Gunter, of a famous London family of confectioners, described these perfumed gum-based sweets as 'a sweetish sort of India-rubber'. Well into the twentieth century, the quality of gums varied. In the 1950s the author Compton MacKenzie recalled that for a penny one could buy one, two or four ounces, but 'we had to be pretty short of pocket money to invest in the last'; however, the best 'were of a quality you could not buy anywhere today – lemon, lime, orange, pear, apple, strawberry, raspberry, apricot . . .'[7]

Manufacturers, too, had mixed feelings about gums. One, in the 1890s, considered that making them was a 'tedious and tiresome process . . . not a profitable undertaking for the small confectioner'.[8] Another, in 1950s America, remarked that huge quantities of cheap gum sweets, never a credit to the industry, were produced from corn syrup, cooking starch and imitation flavours. The best were made from gum arabic, and 'once the customer buys them he will go out of his way to find them again.'[9] They sold fast in USA summers.

The best known (and marketed) in Britain were Fruit Gums (no longer made) – hard, translucent and shiny, and companion products to Fruit Pastilles, discs of chewy paste with a crunchy surface of candied sugar. Products of the Rowntree company, both were devised in the late nineteenth century with the help of French confectioner Claude Gaget.

As the twentieth century wore on, the relationship of gums to fruit grew less direct. In Britain they evolved varieties shaped as miniatures of the elaborate gelatine-set fruit jellies of the nineteenth-century dessert table, or 'winegums', temperance sweets with the names of spirits stamped on them, an edible joke. German childhoods feature Gummi bears,

Advertisement for Rowntree's Fruit Gums, 1952, a classic image from mid-20th-century Britain.

devised in the 1930s by the Haribo company. These *Tanzbären*, 'dancing bears', were a huge success in Europe, although they were not produced in the USA until the 1980s. British children, though, eat jelly babies, tiny anthropomorphic figures in a variety of colours and fruit flavours.

Gums, or gummies (in North America), now range in texture from soft and melting to distinctly tough. Gummy

Publicity caravan for Haribo candies in Quiévy, France, during the 2015 Tour de France.

sweets change with the obsessions of the age, from soft jewel-coloured drops for small children, Canadian jubes (a reference to the jujube of the historic confectionery counter), to house-of-horrors snakes, rats and spiders. Gummi vitamins are designed for fussy children who dislike vitamin pills. Manufacturers nudge their recipes in one direction or another to appeal to different audiences. Southeast Asian companies make bird's-nest-flavoured gums. The recent development of 3D printing as a method for shaping gum-based candies is another step in the long road for shaping novelties.[10]

Turkish delight is a more traditional form of gelled candy. Plain or studded with nuts, flavoured with flower or citrus-scented oils, white with kaymak (clotted cream) or dusted with coconut, it is known in Turkey as *loukum*. This derives from the phrase *rahatü'l-hulkum*, meaning 'ease the throat', and implies its supposedly soothing qualities, though this may have been more of a marketing point than an actual quality of the confection. *Loukum* confused visitors to eighteenth- and nineteenth-century Istanbul: some considered it perfumed and delicious but others could not bring themselves to taste it. The distinctive texture was confusing. The vital ingredient that produces this is wheat starch, integral to Middle Eastern food traditions. Though European confectioners discovered this, they found the candy exceptionally difficult to produce. In 1901, the French artist and writer Pretaxat Lecomte wrote that 'handling . . . must be very skillful and very meticulous, it is in this that all the secret lies, and it should not be thought that this is a minor matter'.[11] Two hours' constant stirring over gentle heat, always in the same direction, was the key in turning starch, water and sugar into *loukum*. Ingredients such as pistachios, clotted cream, musk or rosewater were added before it was poured into wooden moulds to cool and set. *Loukum* was always made with sugar; possible precedents, such as *sucuk*, strings of nuts coated with starch-thickened grape molasses, had a strong flavour.

The stirring process defeated European confectioners. In Britain, they settled on isinglass or gelatine to set their products, and Turkish delight became a cloying translucent paste, as Edmund discovered when he ate too much of it in *The Lion, the Witch and the Wardrobe*. Rose-, lemon- or crème-de-menthe-flavoured, in round wooden boxes full of powdered sugar, or as a filling for a popular chocolate bar, it bears little resemblance to the products of Turkish confectioners. Curiously, proper Turkish delight became a speciality of the Irish city of Cork, where Hadji Bey, an Armenian, settled in the early twentieth century.

One very important global sector of confectionery simply didn't exist until the 1870s. Chewing gum is 'made of any number of cohesive and sticky substances that people chew but do not swallow'.[12] Completely American in origin, it has penetrated all corners of the globe. It provokes strong reactions

– loved by many, a form of currency among children in poor countries, hated by others. In Singapore, it is banned, except for types with therapeutic value.

Chewing meditatively seems to be a human habit. Birch bark tar, mastic (from the tree *Pistacia lentiscus*) and pine tree resin have all been used. By the end of the first millennium, the Mayans of the Yucatan were chewing *chicle* from sapodilla trees. Waxes also provided chews. White Mountain paraffin wax, sold as a household product, was bought by consumers for this in the nineteenth century (wax candies in fantasy shapes filled with syrup are still made in the USA).

Change came in the 1860s. A ton of *chicle* was sent by Antonio Lopez de Santa Ana (former Mexican president and conqueror at the Alamo) from Mexico to his friend Thomas Adams in Manhattan. The idea was to find an industrial application for the gum. By 1871 Adams and his son, inspired by observing the purchase of paraffin wax for chewing, had a patent and a

Confectioners cutting up *loukum* into pieces for sale, Safranbolu, Turkey.

product, individually wrapped balls of unflavoured *chicle* sold as Adams New York No. 1 Chewing Gum. Peppermint-flavoured gum followed in 1879, devised by one William White, and in 1898 William Wrigley Jr started a factory in Chicago. Wrigley was a brilliant promoter, his products including the iconic brands Juicy Fruit (1893) and Doublemint (1914). Chewing gum had well and truly arrived, and its spread around the world became associated with globalization and the idea of North American culture.

Hugely popular with consumers, but the despair of cleaners and civic authorities the world over, chewing gum has managed to maintain an image of American glamour while simultaneously developing local nuances in flavour – strawberry, lemon, jasmine, mangosteen – and packaging. Sometimes gum can be transnational, for example, 'Roma brand cardamom-flavor tablets from Guatemala are popular throughout the Arab-speaking world.'[13] The idea that chewing gum aids relaxation is common. Most of all among candies, chewing gum has developed into versions that claim to be actively good for the teeth. Dentyne is one of the best-known brands.

Bubblegum, or 'blibber-blubber', was first devised in 1906.[14] However, its current form had to wait until 1928, when Walter Deimer, a young employee of the Frank H. Fleer Corporation (also responsible for Chiclets), developed a variety that didn't stick to the skin when the bubble exploded. He put in the first food colouring that came to hand, red, and ever since, pink has been the 'traditional' colour for bubblegum, a candy which truly has to be the ultimate in the 'play with your food' category to which most confections belong, a source of much pleasure to children around the world.

5

Manufacturers and Consumers

In 1597 John Gerard said that the juice of sugar cane produced a 'most pleasant and profitable Sweet called Sugar, whereof is made infinite confections' but that he would not detail them, as his book was not 'a Confectionary, a Sugar Bakers furnace, a Gentlewoman's preserving pan, nor yet an Apothecaries shop or a Dispensatorie'.[1] This mildly disdainful statement is telling, listing those associated with making confections, and both looking back and anticipating the future.

The past belonged to apothecaries who developed sugarwork in medieval Asia and Europe for a wealthy audience. Working through guilds and the secret knowledge of crafts, they were men practising a trade. Guilds were especially powerful in places such as Ottoman Turkey, limiting the activities of individuals but providing craftsmen who were extremely skilled at producing specific confections. From the nineteenth century onwards the medicinal aspect of confectionery was replaced by the pharmaceutical industry, although it is still recalled in cough sweets, breath-freshening chewing gum and TicTacs.

The 'gentlewoman's preserving pan' indicates a subtle thread of female involvement in confectionery. Gerard was specifically referring to a fad for sugarwork among wealthy

English women especially apparent when he was writing. Many seventeenth-century English cookery books include sections on sweetmeats. In North America, Martha Washington's *Booke of Sweetmeats* reflects this tradition.

Poorer women earned money from confectionery. Elizabeth Raffald was an eighteenth-century English example who ran her own shop and catering business. At this time, Quaker women of English origin sold sugarwork for dinner tables in Philadelphia, and Eliza Leslie included recipes for sweetmeats in her books in the nineteenth century. In the Catholic world, convents generated income by selling sweetmeats such as *frutti di Martorana* or *mazápan de Toledo*.

Sweet-making became a female pastime again around 1900. It 'is fairly hard work, but . . . a soother to strained nerves and sad hearts', wrote May Whyte.[2] (Ideas about hygiene were different then: the frontispiece reveals that 'Tootles, a faithful attendant in the sweetroom', was a dog.) Home-made candy was also a fashion in the USA.

Large-scale candy making was heavy work and women generally did not develop industrial businesses. One exception

Josefa de Óbidos, *Still-life with Sweets*, c. 1676, oil on canvas. This artist painted several images of confectionery, perhaps convent sweets, showing elaborate presentations featuring ornamental skewers, ribbons and cut paper.

in the UK was Mary Ann Craven, whose company, founded in 1865, survived as a brand into the 1990s. North American companies Fanny Farmer, Fanny May, Laura Secord and See's (named for Mary See) 'were built by men who used the image of motherly home-made candy . . . to sell their mass-manufactured product'.[3]

The future of sweets lay with the 'confectionery'. Confectioners were men with a repertoire of skills, at the highest level working in 'offices', specialist kitchen areas in large households. They arranged sumptuous desserts, organizing everything – table linen, sugar sculptures, theatricals. Lower down the scale they were tradesmen with shops and businesses. Attitudes towards them were ambiguous. As Robert Campbell said in 1747, 'It requires no small Knowledge to

Robert Frederick Blum, *The Ameya*, c. 1893, oil on canvas. Blum painted a number of Japanese street scenes; this one shows a traditional sugarworker blowing warm syrup to make sugar ornaments, fascinating his audience of young women and children.

compleat a Confectioner, though I never esteem him one of the most useful Members of Society.'[4]

French court confectioners were influential, producing important books such as those by François Massialot and Menon. *Le Cannameliste français* (1751) by Joseph Gilliers included impressive plates for rococo dessert layouts, illustrating an important aspect of the confectioner's remit. Gilliers worked for royalty, as did Nicolas Stohrer, whose establishment in Paris still exists, reflecting the patisserie and outside catering aspects of the confectioner's work. In London, James Gunter gave his name to an eighteenth-century business that survived into the 1950s.

North American skills were augmented by migrant confectioners of German descent, and numerous Italians worked in the trade in Vienna. In London, William Jarrin, originally from the Parma area, detailed his skills in *The Italian Confectioner* (1820), leaving an unsurpassed record of now extinct skills relating to sugar sculpture. His contemporary Antonin Carême also left a book illustrating architectural fantasies in sugar but giving less practical detail.

The craft was also an opportunity for anyone with a few pounds of sugar and a boiling pan. Examples include *franfellicaro,* street confectioners shown in Italian prints, the Japanese *ameya* captured in a painting by American artist Robert Frederick Blum in the 1890s, and street sellers interviewed in mid-nineteenth-century London by Henry Mayhew, whose workshops were small, dark and often underground. In some countries confectionery production remains an integral part of street life, for instance in India, where halvais prepare confections in front of passers-by, the sights and aromas acting as their own advertisement.

The twentieth-century future lay in mass production. Declining sugar prices and increased mechanization were a general pattern in both Western Europe and North America. Traditional flavours and colours were substituted by industrially produced ones. The Great Exhibition of 1851 had a significant impact.

Chocolate developed as an industrial competitor for sugar through entrepreneurs. Some, such as Joseph Terry (who acquired control of a confectionery business in 1828), Sprüngli (Switzerland, established 1845) and Whitman's (USA, 1842), were already confectioners. Croft, of Wilbur & Croft (USA), was already a confectioner in 1865 when the two formed a company. Milton S. Hershey, already successful with the Lancaster Caramel Company in the 1880s, sold it in 1894 to concentrate on making chocolate. Frank C. Mars founded the company that became Mars Inc. in 1920.

In the UK Cadbury's was founded in 1824 and Rowntree's in 1862, both selling tea, coffee and chocolate. J. S. Fry & Sons, always chocolate processors, were founded in 1822. Philippe Suchard (France) trained as a confectioner but was principally interested in chocolate, founding a company in 1826. Swiss chocolatier Rodolphe Lindt founded his company in 1879 and Henri Nestlé began as a milk processor in 1867.

Chocolate manufacturers used bright packaging and advertising to lend allure to their dark-coloured products, and brand names to assure quality. Sugar confectionery and chocolate met in countlines such as Mars Bars and Kit Kats, bars sold by number, not weight. The North American term 'candy bar', hinting at the filling, rather than the UK 'chocolate bar', suggesting the coating, may more truly reflect the relative proportions of the confections involved. Some companies used their acumen to develop sugar-based lines such as Rowntree's Fruit Gums.

The sugar confectionery industry had lower entry costs and small companies could maintain a presence. Whims and

Boiling pans, perhaps containing syrup or fruit purées, at the Rowntree's factory in York, UK, 1890s.

fashions were increasingly important, putting a new spin on items made by old techniques. Branding was less easy for generic products such as barley sugar. The twentieth-century history of sugar confectionery was one of increasing concentration, as large companies (often chocolate-based) acquired smaller ones or merged. In the UK, Trebor, already merged with liquorice producers Bassett's, and Pascalls, Maynards and Craven-Keiller were all subsumed by Cadbury's. In the USA, Leaf Brand (founded in the 1920s) became a company with a portfolio of names such as Jolly Rancher (established in 1949). Leaf's USA brands were acquired by Hershey in the 1990s. Chewing gum, which offered opportunities for Thomas Adams, William Wrigley and many others, was subject to mergers and takeovers. Haribo, founded by Hans Rigel Senior in

1922 and still independent, made clear gum sweets a German favourite and has itself acquired other companies.

Sugar confectionery remained a fragmented industry with a wide range of products, the largest suppliers – Kraft, Cadbury Schweppes and Hershey – accounting for only 23 per cent of sales around the millennium year.[5] One company whose name did not appear until 2012, but was named second from the top (just behind Mars Inc.) in the world's confectionery companies in 2013, was Mondelēz International, a multinational, formerly part of Kraft Foods, which itself had swallowed such brands as Terry, Suchard, Cadbury and Chiclets.[6]

Sugar confectionery had an advantage over chocolate in that it was both an established product and beautiful to look at. Display is part of the lure of sweets and candies, from sugar models in the processions of medieval caliphs to the multicoloured jars of sweetshop shelves. Evidence for how sweets were displayed in the sixteenth and seventeenth centuries can be seen in the work of many still-life painters. Juan van der Hamen y León (1596–1631) depicted Spanish confections including *túrron* and small twisted white rings, possibly of pulled sugar. Josefa de Óbidos (*c.* 1630–1684) also left detailed images, perhaps of Portuguese convent sweets: red and white comfits, elaborate paste, gingerbread or cookie-type products enhanced with elaborately beribboned decorative skewers and fringed paper. In his paintings, Luis Meléndez (1716–1780) showed practical wooden boxes (of a type still used for fruit pastes) that hinted at hidden riches. Their successors were elaborate cardboard gift boxes for fondants and chocolates, and decorative toffee tins. Gold-leaf-enhanced sugar and fruit paste has been replaced by foil wrappers in the developed world, though *vark*, edible silver leaf, is still used in India.

Hero's recruiting at Kelsey's; — or — Guard-Day at St James's.

James Gillray, *Hero's Recruiting at Kelsey's*, 1797, hand-coloured etching.
Satirical print depicting a lean, elderly officer and a commissioned
youngster eating comfits and ice cream in Kelsey's, a fashionable
London confectioner's. A third soldier stands guard, or perhaps acts
as a lookout.

In the late seventeenth century Nicolas de l'Armessin depicted *La Confiseuse* in a fantasy costume of flat circular boxes labelled with the names of regional specialities, sugar loaves and swags of fruit. She holds a triangular tiered stand supporting bowls of small confections – a pyramidal arrangement of confectionery, fashionable at the time. To her side are a shop counter and shelves carrying more boxes.

The best eighteenth-century confectioner's shops were fitted out with mirrors and gilt, confections displayed in clear glass jars placed to catch the light in the window, interspersed with fresh fruit such as oranges and pineapples. Late eighteenth- and early nineteenth-century prints illustrate shops, their staff (who generally seem to be attractive young women), customers and stock. This is the point at which the notion of the bow window full of sugary treats of the 'old-fashioned sweetshop' began to evolve, an ideal subsequently aided by depictions in advertising, though lots of confectionery must have been sold from street stalls and vendors.

Until the early nineteenth century, much of the confectionery on sale was probably made in the shop, but manufacture rapidly industrialized and retailing developed as an increasingly important activity in its own right. Sweets and candies became treats associated with the sale of other sundries, such as tobacco and newspapers, developing shops classed as CTNs (confectioner-tobacconist-newsagents). Small general stores, grocers and chain stores such as Woolworths all sold sweets and candy as specialist confectioners became increasingly rare. Fragile glass containers, which simultaneously protected and displayed preserved fruit or boiled sweets, were increasingly replaced by clear cellophanes or plastics. The second half of the twentieth century brought retailing opportunities undreamt of in the past, such as supermarkets and the Internet, which now provide outlets for vast quantities of candy.

Anon., *The Taste of Today*, *c.* 1802, hand-coloured etching published by Aaron Martinet. This satirical print shows the interior of a confectioner's shop with fashionably dressed clients.

Who buys and consumes all these sweets? Although initially an expensive and precious preserve of the wealthy, sugary foods became pleasing trivialities as the price of ingredients fell. A persistent theme of women and children as consumers of confectionery becomes apparent from quite early on and is well established by the nineteenth century. The shop run by Farrance was described in a guide to eating out in London in 1815:

> in this temple Pomona and Ceres hold daily a levee of
> beauty and fashion . . . you may observe at all hours in
> the forenoon a whole nidus of little Cupids and Psyches
> feasting in terrene nectar and ambrosia. In plainer terms,
> ladies generally regale their younger friends and relatives
> here with the incomparable bon-bons.[7]

Georges Achille-Fould, *Boy Selling Barley Sugar*, from an issue of *L'Illustration* of 1891. A sentimental image of a child selling barley sugar on the street. He is remarkably clean and well-dressed: contemporary photographs indicate much harder lives.

Images and graphics show those who were attracted by the fantasy displays in confectioner's shop windows, including the young and the poor. Confectionery impressed the naive.

The attraction of confectionery for children has long been implicit in Western culture. In 1608, moulded marzipan conceits were said to be 'excellent good to please children'.[8] Local confectioners and small shops must always have had a few cheap items for sale to youngsters. And in early nineteenth-century England, what small boy could resist Wellington pillars or Gibraltar rock? Later in the century, advertising (for instance that for Fry's) played on this with depictions of children buying sweets, and many autobiographies, such as those by Roald Dahl, mention favourite childhood indulgences.

Children, especially lower-class ones, were significant consumers of cheap sweets and penny candies, which in late nineteenth-century cities offered escapism and comfort in poverty-stricken lives, 'infinite fantasy worlds in addition to something delectable to eat'.[9] From this time on the industry was built on their ever-changing preferences, in which innovation is everything. Candy, always slightly divorced from reality, became ever more fantastic. Names of early twentieth-century North American items illustrate this: Monster Tubes, Eagle Twists, Electric Light Wires, Sphinx Package, Scorcher.[10] The confectionery industry in Britain was equally unhinged, and one author, inspired by the idea 'of compiling a definitive alphabetical list of every sweet, ice-lolly, chocolate bar and bubblegum that ever existed in Britain', found this an impossible task.[11]

For children, confectionery provided, and still provides, lessons in relationships between money and power. The sweet-shop, the candy store, the Australian lolly counter, is a place where children learn about 'value, saving, addiction, sharing, and credit'.[12] Late nineteenth-century print media included the notion of power in confectionery advertisements. 'See their eyes as she buys Fry's' was one tag line, promoting the notion of envy among young consumers. Protracted deliberation over the choices teaches how to be good consumers. Stevan Dohanos's *Saturday Morning Post* cover in 1944, showing a small boy considering a candy display while the shop owner's face glazes over with boredom, made the point visually. Print and packaging extended this over the decades, merging into film and television. Character merchandising, film and TV tie-ins and interactive confectionery combined with toys have been signposted as ways for the industry to maintain interest from their young customers in the twenty-first century.

For women, confectioners provided public space in which it was socially acceptable to meet and enjoy sweet foods, as in the nineteenth-century shops of the Viennese confectioners. In North America some candy advertising was aimed specifically at adult women, especially that relating to more expensive and luxurious confections involving chocolate and fondant. Described collectively as bonbons, their composition and name implied French cachet, and advertising hinted at sensual, decadent enjoyment. An association between ornamental and inessential sugary foods and abstract notions of sweetness and femininity was apparent in North America at this time. The notion of sweets and candies as special treats for women still applies, though the association is now skewed towards chocolates. These were heavily advertised as gifts, particularly from men to women, for much of the twentieth century, and still are.

Owing to the lack of sharp differentiation between sweets and candy and other forms of sweet food, it is less easy to generalize about them away from Western Europe and North America. But in one major culture of sweetness, that of India, things are different. Sweet foods and confections have a special place here, because they often include ghee, a substance that acts as a purifier of foods within India's highly stratified caste system. In turn this makes their products acceptable to all, even members of the highest caste.[13] This means they are acceptable food for all travellers and as gifts between lower and higher castes, and the confectioner, although not of the highest caste, is a respectable individual. Unusually, sweets also have an association with masculinity, especially in Bengal where they are given as presents to men on two special days, *Bhaiphonta* (when girls give their male siblings sweets) and *Jamai Sasthi* (when fathers-in-law give sons-in-law presents). Sweet foods, too, are offered to the gods, and Ganesh, the elephant-headed god, is often depicted holding a *laddu*.

Statistics, inevitably relating to industrial producers, show that in the early twenty-first century, the global confectionery market was valued at U.S.$88.7 billion. Of this, chocolate accounted for 54 per cent, sugar for 34 per cent and gum for the remaining 12 per cent. By volume, the relative proportions were reversed. Of a total volume of just over 14 million tonnes, sugar confectionery production accounted for 52 per cent, chocolate for 40 per cent and gum for 8 per cent.[14] Chocolate is relatively expensive to buy, so sugar, often very cheap, is more popular in developing countries; in hot climates, it also keeps better.

In terms of consumption, North America provided the largest market both by volume and value for sugar confectionery. Per head, North Americans accounted for 6.6 kg of sugar confectionery each a year (figures exceeded only by some Scandinavian countries such as Sweden and Denmark), and the inhabitants of the UK for 5 kg per person. All these countries also had significant per capita consumption of chocolate confectionery. Western Europe generally was an important market, second behind North America in value terms, but third in volume. The inhabitants of the Far East, especially the

Chinese, who have experienced rapidly rising incomes, buy more confectionery by volume, but pay less for it than Western Europeans do.[15] Chewing gum, though, is important in the Japanese market.

Confectionery consumption is not the same as total sugar consumption. The latter is much higher: in 2012 Americans were reckoned to consume about 128 lb (58 kg) of added sugar per head per year.[16] In the UK sugar consumption steadied at about 88 lb (39 kg) a year, having grown 'five-fold in the hundred years after 1835' and risen 'extremely rapidly between 1950 and 1960' to a total consumption 126 lb (just over 57 kg) per person per year.[17] The rise in the 1950s was a reaction to tight rationing during and after the Second World War.

Sugar is added, in many different forms, to all sorts of foods. It is an ingredient used in vast quantities in soft drinks and added to a huge range of manufactured food, sweet and savoury, not just as ordinary sucrose, but in many guises – glucose, dextrose, high-fructose corn syrup, honey, maltose and many others.

Sweets and candy, defined by the presence of sugar even if they account for a relatively small proportion of it in the diet, are inevitably prominent in a wider discussion about sugar in relation to health. This has emerged as a significant factor in attitudes to confectionery in the last fifty years. Well before this, doubts were expressed about sugar and dental health even in the sixteenth century when a visitor to England noted that the English had bad teeth 'from their too great use of sugar'.[18] Confectionery was the subject of moral panics in the nineteenth century, especially cheap items bought by the poor, and Britain's public-health scandals related to sweets helped establish consumer protection laws.

High sugar consumption generally has inspired debates about adverse effects on health since the 1970s, when John

Camille Boutet, *We Will Know How to Sacrifice*, 1918, colour lithograph. This print was made at the end of the First World War, a time of sugar shortages in many countries.

Yudkin, a professor of nutrition, examined evidence for links between sugar consumption and dental caries, diabetes and coronary heart disease in *Pure, White and Deadly*. More recently, endocrinologist Robert Lustig, concerned with rising obesity levels in North America, looked at sugar consumption in relation to health in *Fat Chance*. He concluded that all added sugar has a deleterious effect, and that high-fructose corn syrup, because of the way it is metabolized in the body, is the worst: 'Our bodies have not adapted to our current environmental sugar glut and it is killing us.'[19]

World Health Organization guidelines in 2015 considered sugar in relation to dental disease and obesity. They strongly recommended that total sugar – from all sources, not just confectionery – should be kept below 10 per cent of total daily energy intake.[20] This works out at 200 to 250 calories a day for a sedentary adult, equivalent to 50 to 60 g of sugar.

Sugar – whether it is high-fructose corn syrup in a can of soft drink, or cane sucrose in the best-quality, most beautifully made artisan candy – is over-abundant and over-consumed. Sweets, with their frivolous, luxurious past and magic associations with health, wealth and happiness, are part of the problem and an obvious target, but in a sense, they are at least honest, wearing their sweetness unashamedly.

6

Sweets and Festivity

An enduring use of sweets and candies is to mark out special days, symbols of good fortune and generosity. Abundance, colour and glitter all increase their attraction, and they help children, especially, to remember the importance of a day or season.

Festive occasions divide roughly into markers of the human life cycle or calendar events. Birth and marriage are universally celebrated with sweetness, and sometimes it appears in relation to death. Calendar events can be religious or secular. During the Muslim fast of Ramadan, when food is permissible only during the hours of darkness, sweets are a welcome source of quick energy, an indulgence with a long history. At the end of the fast, *Eid-el-Fitr* involves celebration and plenty, including numerous sweets. In Christian countries, the festival of Easter has preserved the celebration of sweetness; the concept of fasting for Lent may have mostly vanished, but Carnival survives in places. Sweets may also mark out Christian saints' days and festivals honouring Indian gods. Christmas, another occasion for sweetness, has both Christian and pagan roots, celebrations of the New Year in various cultures anticipate good things to come with confectionery.

J. Robyn, *St Nicholas's Day*, 18th century, print. A group of Dutch children on St Nicholas's Day with traditional gifts of dolls, gingerbread and letter shapes made of confectionery pastes including marzipan and sugar paste.

Display and generosity run deep. Constructions made of sweets or candies were sometimes demolished and distributed to participants or witnesses in early modern Europe. This sometimes ended in food fights as the sweetmeats were flung about, as at a banquet witnessed by John Evelyn in London in 1667.[1] On a more decorous level, the seventeenth-century French confectioner Massialot described how, at desserts for fraternities, there was a decorative basket for each guest, commonly adorn'd with small Ribbands, and Taffaty Covers . . . and fill'd up with all Sorts of Sweet-Meats, Biskets, March-panes, Orange and Lemon Faggots, dry'd Fruits &c. so that the most delicious Comfits may lye at the Top . . . Every individual Person shuts up, and takes away his Basket, to treat his Family and Friends at Home.[2]

Wedding favours and children's party bags have a long precedent.

Cast sugar provides some eye-catching objects, especially as the *muertos* of the Mexican Day of the Dead (2 November). Pale, bone-like, lavishly decorated with Day-Glo sugar icing (sometimes spelling the name of the recipient), their hollow eye sockets glow with metallic coloured paper. Remarkably exuberant, they are a startling celebration of death in a world increasingly shy of the subject. They also continue the medieval tradition of cast-sugar ornaments, and are sold at *la feria*

Muertos, skulls cast from hard sugar and decorated with coloured icing and foil, made for *Día de los Muertos*, the Mexican Day of the Dead.

del alfeñique, a name that reflects the distant past of worked sugar as *fanid* or *phanita*. Other shapes feature, too, often made from sugar paste: angels, babies in coffins, hearts, animals, hats, guitars – a random list just like that in a seventeenth-century book of sugarwork. *Muertos* are a fusion of Spanish sugarworking techniques, the Christian festivals of All Saints and All Souls and a pre-existing Native American cult of ancestor worship.

Europeans also remember the dead at this time, especially in Italy, where *ossi dei morti* (bones of the dead) appear in the shops. Cast-sugar figures, made by techniques similar to those in Mexico, appear for the Sicilian Day of the Dead festivals as knights on horseback, dancers or other designs. Marzipan *frutti di Martorana* are a feature of this day as well, gifts from the dead. Cast sugar also reappears again at Sicilian Easters, in more seasonal shapes such as lambs.

North American Halloween may or may not echo the feasts of the Day of the Dead, but 'trick or treat' reached its current form only in the mid-twentieth century. A form of

Pupi de cena, cast-sugar images made for All Saints Day, Sicily.

Georg Flegel, *Still-life with Parrot*, *c.* 1630, oil on copper. The parrot presides over a lavish dessert setting including fresh fruit, biscuits and a tazza containing several types of comfit.

it was established before the Second World War, but 'by the 1950s food manufacturers and retailers were figuring out ways to cash in with commercial foods.'[3] A combination of these interests, plus a desire to minimize the hooliganism that had become part of the evening in earlier decades, was exploited by confectionery manufacturers in packaging candy specially for this time.

Comfits and dragées have a long association with birth and marriage celebrations, and with Carnival. Nuts and seeds used as centres symbolize fertility, and their manufacture, each sugar coat increasing their size, provides a graphic illustration of increase. Symbolizing wealth and fecundity, they are still given away as favours in many other places, just as sugar almonds were always part of Renaissance banquets, to be carried away in pockets and handkerchiefs by the guests.

Especially important in France, they are associated with the important life events, communicating joy and celebration. At christenings, they are traditionally purchased by the godfather and distributed to guests by the parents, following a careful hierarchy of presentation. This is an old tradition: in *The Batchelar's Banquet* (a translation of the *Quinze joies de mariage*), the narrator bewails the cost of 'Sugar, Biskets, Comphets and Carowayes, Marmilade and martchpaine . . . all kind of sweete suckets, and superfluous banqueting stuffe' to be provided for the gossips (female friends of the mother) at a lying-in.[4]

Comfits were popular on social occasions in Ottoman Turkey, eaten with sherbet or wine, a custom that was widespread over time and history in both the Islamic world and Europe. They were served at birth and circumcision celebrations and were thrown over the bride at weddings; similar customs were found elsewhere, for instance in Afghanistan where *noql* appear at weddings and engagements.

Italian *confetto*, meaning a small sweet, gave the word 'confetti' as a collective term for these. Comfits were also thrown at Carnival in Italy, something recorded in the eighteenth century by Goethe (who observed that the 'sweets' were actually sometimes plaster imitations) and in the nineteenth by William Gunter, who also said that nonpareils were mixed with other comfits for New Year's Day in France and Italy, where 'Every BEAU is expected to present to *all* his lady acquaintance, a packet of *Dragêts*, saluting her at the same time as his reward.'[5] A larger hollow comfit could hold a small gift, perhaps an early

Clara Peeters, *Still-life with Tart, Porcelain, Silver Tazza with Sweets, and Oysters*, *c.* 1612–13, oil on panel. The disc in the centre of this picture may be a tart but is possibly a circular marchpane, used for celebrating special occasions. It is strewn with tiny coloured comfits and decorated with sprigs of rosemary, one of which carries small gold charms; this form of decoration suggests a wedding context.

precursor of the packaged chocolate Easter egg. The change to paper confetti took place in late nineteenth-century France, but smaller egg-shaped sugar comfits or pieces of chocolate are still panned with sugar coatings for this festival.

In British customs, fruitcakes signify festivity, especially weddings, but the true indicator was originally the icing and marzipan, descendant of the iced marchpane of the seventeenth century. These were garnished 'with prettie conceipts' cast in moulds. 'Sticke long comfits upright in it, cast bisket and carrowaies in it,' said Sir Hugh Platt in 1609. The 'conceits' were variously shaped, 'letters, knots, Armes, escocheons, beasts, birds, and other fancies'.[6] A rosemary branch, hung with gold charms, distinguished wedding marchpanes in early modern northern Europe.[7] In the play *Women Beware Women* (1657), a ram and the bull, symbols of lust, appear on a zodiac-decorated marchpane.

Thick marzipan discs moulded with decorative patterns are still made in modern Germany for special occasions, painted with coloured motifs and greetings, bases dipped in chocolate. The paste is also modelled as figures – fruit, vegetables, hearts, angels and Santa Claus. Marzipan pigs are symbols of good luck and plenty in northern Europe. 'In Holland in December, almost every counter houses several kilos of moulded pink pig or piglet, whose size diminishes as people buy a piece from snout to tail.'[8]

In Britain, sugar icing developed as an art form. Materials varied with fashion: sugar paste, royal icing, inedible plaster, metal, plastic, ribbons, fantasies of piped icing, silvering or gilding. White, always symbolic of purity in Europe and a

German birthday 'cake', 2002, a moulded disc of marzipan decorated with hand-painting in edible colours and partially dipped in chocolate.

major attraction of sugar, was seldom departed from in this scheme until a few decades ago, when colours became acceptable. Wedding cakes are for sharing and guests carry pieces away. In mid-twentieth-century Britain it was quite usual to send portions in special boxes by post to absent friends.

At Christmas, decorated cakes are now eaten on 25 December, but originally belonged to Twelfth Night (6 January). Always heavily decorated, often with moulded sugar-paste figures, they were the focus of many games and rituals.

Sugar paste was used for courtly work from the Renaissance onwards, and embellished tables, marchpanes and other confectionery. It has excellent sculptural qualities and, modelled freehand, imagination, skill and cost were the only limits on what could be produced. Moulds were also used. Those surviving from the eighteenth century include ones for making sugar-paste models of beds to ornament wedding cakes, but overt symbols of matrimony were replaced in the nineteenth century by symbolic devices – birds, garlands, sheaves of wheat and austere sprays of flowers. Figures representing the bride and groom became a twentieth-century tradition. Moulds were used on other occasions. A surviving set of French moulds from the late eighteenth century to the 1830s includes patterns for making tiny sugar baskets, fruits to fill them, and little dogs, crowns or hats to sit on cushions (also moulded from sugar paste), probably used as favours. Larger moulds include royal ciphers, dolphins for supporting displays, and ones for items such as obelisks and military trophies.[9]

Moulded sugar holds infinite appeal for children. Clear sugar toys were a feature of Christmas for Pennsylvania Dutch children in the late nineteenth and early twentieth centuries. On Christmas Eve they "'set their plates" . . . During the night, Christ-Kindle, also known as *Grisch-Kindel*, or Christ Child, brought gifts for good boys and girls . . . nuts, an apple

Janes Fine Confectionery, Washington, DC, *c.* 1919–20. The little girl is holding a striped candy cane, suggesting this image was taken close to Christmas.

or an orange, and clear toy candy.'[10] This was a product of blended traditions of British and German settlers. As *roter Zuckerhase*, hare shapes cast in red sugar, clear toy candy is also an Easter tradition in southern Germany.

Christmas in North America is generally marked with pulled sugar-candy canes. The start of their association with this festival is unclear, but belongs to the wider tradition of eye-catching novelties made using special skills. In Britain, pulled sugar, in all its exuberant glory, stands for holidays, souvenirs of the seaside breaks that developed as respite for industrial workers in the late nineteenth century.

Southern European Christmases and Easters feature nougat. In Spain, '*Turrón* . . . is eaten in awe-inspiring amounts in the festive period surrounding Christmas,' stocked in huge slabs in the *confiterías*.[11] At the Seville Easter Fair it caught the eye of an early twentieth-century English cookery writer: 'There are rows of stalls where "turron" is sold . . . and it is brown, or white, or pink, or any colour of the rainbow.'[12] The Spanish exported the custom and the sweet elsewhere, so that as far away as the Philippines, flat tins and boxes of *turrón* also came to represent Christmas. Italian *torrone* shares these festive associations, and also appears for occasions such as the Feast of San Gennaro, held annually in New York's Little Italy. *Gaz,* the Middle Eastern variety of nougat, is a traditional sweet for *Nouw Roz,* New Year in Persia and Afghanistan, a festival that occurs in late March or early April, as winter turns to spring. In Afghanistan it appears along with sugar-candy, little chickpea cookies and *toot shrini* ('mulberry sweets') moulded from almond paste. Another New Year confection is *Khasta-el-shireen*, large discs of caramelized almond or apricot kernels, 'a common sight in the bazaars . . . a special treat, especially for children, at festival times such as Nauroz (New Year) and Eid'.[13]

Egg-yolk confections have links with weddings. The nineteenth-century British author George Borrow left a remarkable description of the use of *yémas* at gypsy weddings in Spain:

> nearly a ton weight of sweetmeats was prepared at extraordinary expense . . . of all kinds, and of all forms, but principally yémas . . . strewn on the floor to a depth of three inches. Into this room . . . tripped the bride and bridegroom, dancing . . .

They were accompanied by their followers, also dancing, and, 'In a few minutes the sweetmeats were reduced to a powder, or rather to a mud, and the dancers were soiled to the knees with sugar, fruits, and the yolks of eggs.'[14]

Four types of egg-yolk sweets, presented with more decorum, are still traditional at Thai weddings. Their golden colour symbolizes material wealth, a sweet marriage, a long and happy life and mutual support.[15]

In India presents of sweets generally are important, conveying many feelings – of gratitude, affection, respect, joy, rewards for attainment. Sweets mark successful exam results, promotion at work, weddings and births. *Laddu* are treats for any celebration and appear at gatherings in the same way as the British might produce a cake. As elsewhere, the intersection of human life events, religious and secular days of celebration and regional tastes in sweetmeats make it impossible to generalize about specific confections. Names and interpretations of festivals also vary, but the overwhelming importance of sweetness is clear. In West Bengal in mid-autumn, Durga Puja, Kali Puja and Diwali, a festival often associated with Lakshmi, goddess of plenty, all follow each other, and all involve various sweet foods. For Kali Puja,

Juan van der Hamen y León, *Still-life with Turrón*, 1622, oil on canvas.

Diwali, a mid-autumn festival in the Hindu year, is celebrated with sweets and light.

Bengali confectioners make *pera* of sugar and reduced milk, 'unhurriedly forming great mounds of sweet paste into disks about the size of a silver dollar . . . The pilgrims, in their festive best, buy these by twos and threes to present to the deity,' each purchase placed in a leaf cone with a brilliant red hibiscus flower.[16]

Sweets are most prominent at Diwali. This, in late October, recalls the victory of good over evil. It features lights, sweets and gift-giving, in traditions reminiscent, to Westerners, of Christmas. At this time, 'animals, gods and goddesses made from sugar (often elegant white and edible sculptures) are sold in the market for children.'[17] Other special days around this time include Bijoya Dashami, the last day of Durga Puja, associated with discarding ill feeling and hostility and visiting relatives and friends. Everyone must be offered sweets that cannot be refused, to the extent that even diabetics will nibble token fragments. Largesse is involved in all these events, and perceptions of a man's prestige may, in part, be derived from observations about the quantity of sweetmeats he serves on festive occasions.

In India sweetness is introduced early in life. Madhur Jaffrey recounted that, in the hour of her birth, her grand-mother 'wrote the sacred syllable Om ("I am")' on her tongue with a finger dipped in fresh honey.[18] Sweets are also a vital part of marriage customs, couples ritually feeding each other with sweets at engagement ceremonies, and as in the Arabic and English languages, notions of love and sweetness are conflated.

Traditions to do with sweets and candy in China are less obvious, but one is associated with Chinese New Year. First recorded in 1585, and still very important, this is the habit of 'sweetening the mouth' of the Kitchen God, whose paper image has watched the family activities for the previous twelve months.[19] 'As an agent of heavenly authority, the Kitchen God spends the whole year with the family, seeing and hear-ing everything.'[20] Immediately before New Year, the family give him offerings of sweet cakes and preserved fruits, or smear the mouth of the image with sweetmeats. The image is then ritually burnt, sending him to heaven, where the sweets will make him give a good report to the other gods.

Viewing the dental havoc wrought by sugar, considering its role as a source of empty calories in the diet and the implica-tions that has for health, nutritionists might wish that sweets could be restricted to bribing gods, or at least to special days and seasons. The efforts of manufacturers to make healthier candy for the twenty-first century, though, is to miss the point. The large and profitable confectionery industry is well aware of this. Sweets and candies are not intended to be a routine

Advertisement for Vittorio Colussi, late 19th or early 20th century.
The image of a woman scattering *biscotti* and candies from the rooftops
to the world references Carnival and illustrates frivolity, generosity and
fun – themes that run through the history of sweets.

part of a healthy diet. They are exuberant and anarchic, halfway between food and fashion, edible toys, symbols of good things. Despite their dark side and deleterious effect on the health of individuals, they have brought colour, fun and frivolity into a serious world for many centuries.

Recipes

To Make a Walnut, that when you cracke it, you shall find Biskets, and Carrawayes in it, or a pretty Posey written

Anon., *A Closet for Ladies and Gentlewomen* (London, 1608)

Take a piece of your Past royall white [sugar paste], being beaten with Gum-tragacant, and mixed with a little searsed Cynnamon, which will bring your past into a Walnut shell colour, then drive it thinne, and cut it into two pieces, and put the one piece into the one halfe of your mould, and the other into the other, then out what you please into the nut, and close the mould together, and so make three or foure Walnuts.

To make Barley Sugar

John Nott, *The Cooks and Confectioners Dictionary 1726*
(London, 1980)

Boil Barley in Water, strain it through a Hair Sieve, then put the Decoction into clarify'd Sugar brought to a caramel height, or the last Degree of Boiling: Then take it off the Fire and let the Boiling settle; then pour it upon a Marble-stone rubb'd with the oil of Olives: when it cools and begins to grow hard, cut it into Pieces, and roll it into Lengths as you please.

To make Sugar-candy

John Nott, *Cooks and Confectioners Dictionary 1726*
(London, 1980)

Boil a Quantity of Sugar till it comes to a *blown* Quality; then put it into an earthern Pot, in which small Sticks are laid a-cross; set the Pot into a Stove, and the Sugar will coagulate about the Sticks.

Some Confectioners pour the Sugar upon those little Sticks, laid upright, cross-wise, or side-wise, and let it stand fourteen or fifteen Days in the Stove, and afterwards pour in hot Water at several times, and then leave them again for a Day, and break the Pot the next Morning, and so find the Sugar-candy round about the Sticks.

Some, having taken away the first Crust, set the rest again into the Stove till another is formed, and so proceed till the whole Work is completed.

Almond Prawlings in Red

William Alexis Jarrin, *The Italian Confectioner* (London, 1820)

1 lb. Almonds, 1 lb. Sugar

Take a pound of almonds, free from dust, dissolve with a little water a pound of sugar, put the almonds in, and boil them with the sugar; when the almonds crack, take them off the fire, stir them to a *sand*, sift them to take off the lose sugar; put back the sugar in a pan on the fire, with a little water; boil it to a *caramel* [hard crack], add your almonds, with a little liquid carmine, stir them till they have taken all the sugar, put them in a sieve, and sprinkle them with a little orange flower water to give them a flavour and make them shine.

English Almond Rock and Hardbake

Henry Weatherley, *A Treatise on the Art of Boiling Sugar*
(Philadelphia, PA, 1865)

To seven pound of raw sugar put three and a half pints of water, boil to the crack, pour it on your slab, and put over it quickly four pounds of picked Barbary almonds, mix them well in; when very firm make it into a thick block, place it on a wooden bench and cut slices off with a long thin sharp knife; it is safer to reduce the above a little if the sugar is strong, or it will grain in the working.

Almond Hardbake

Lay your split almonds on your slab or frames, round or any other shape, proceed as in the last boil, and when the sugar is done pour thinly over.

[Suggested quantities for a small batch: 500 g light soft brown sugar, 250 ml water, 300 g blanched whole almonds.]

Vanilla Caramels No. 1 Quality American recipe

E. Skuse, *Skuse's Complete Confectioner,* 10th edn (London, *c.* 1900)

6 lbs sugar
2 quarts sweet cream
1 ½ lbs fresh butter
4 lbs glucose
essence of vanilla

Put the sugar, glucose, and cream in the pan; put on a slow fire and stir constantly; let boil to a stiff ball, then add the butter; keep stirring, and when it has well boiled through, remove the pan from the fire. Flavour with vanilla essence. Pour out on oiled plate; when set, mark with caramel cutter; when cold, divide with sharp knife and wrap each caramel in waxed paper.

[Suggested quantities for a small batch: 500 g sugar, 280 ml single cream, 150 g butter, 280 g glucose syrup.]

Salt Water Taffy Kisses
White, Pink and Chocolate for Counter Pans
Charles Apell, *Twentieth Century Candy Teacher* (USA: place not given, 1912)

30 lbs. glucose
20 lbs. sugar
1 qt. of water
1 lb. of flour
1 lb. of Nucoa butter
1 lb. of creamery butter

Cook to a crack in stirrer kettle. . . . Add 2 oz. of vanilla, 4 oz. of salt and pour out onto a greased cold slab, and when cool enough to handle, pull on machine and always pull your soft boiled goods as cold as possible on the machine and they will be easy to handle on the table when spinning out your batch, as the colder you run them out the better shape your kisses will have when wrapped.

[Suggested quantities for a small batch: 750 g glucose syrup, 500 g sugar, 100 ml water, 25 g flour, 50 g vegetable cooking fat, a few drops vanilla essence, 1 teaspoon salt.]

Engagement Favours
Robert Wells, *The Bread and Biscuit Baker's and Sugar Boiler's Assistant* (London, 1896)

Break up 1 lb. of loaf sugar into small particles, let it dissolve in a pan with ½ pint of water and 2 spoonfuls of lemon juice; skim and boil to the ball, add pieces of lemon peel tied together with a string, boil until sample is brittle; take out the lemon peel, pour out the sugar onto an oiled slab, taking care to distribute it so that the whole mass cools at the same time. It is pulled, manipulated and cut in the ordinary way. A small part of the sugar coloured red and boiled separately may be used to variegate the sweets, and should be worked in just before cutting.

Treacle Toffee
May Whyte, *High-class Sweetmaking* (Birkenhead, *c.* 1910)

1 lb. treacle
1 lb. yellow moist sugar
large half teacupful cold water
fourth of a teaspoonful cream of tartar

Put in pan butter, treacle, sugar and water, and dissolve in usual way, stirring all the time; add the cream of tartar when it boils, and boil, stirring constantly and carefully to 260° Fahrenheit. Then pour onto a buttered slab, between buttered candy bars, or pour into a buttered tin, and when half-cold score into squares. Break up when cold and wrap in waxed paper.

Nougat Montelimart
Louisa Thorpe, *Bonbons and Simple Sugar Sweets* (London, 1922)

8 whites of eggs
2½ gills water
½ lb. blanched, dried and chopped almonds
¼ lb. glacé cherries
2 lb. loaf sugar
¼ lb. white honey
¼ lb. blanched pistachio nuts
a little orange-flower water
a pinch of cream of tartar

Put the sugar and water in a saucepan and place it over gentle heat. While it is dissolving cut up the almonds, nuts and cherries into small pieces. Place some bars on a slab lined with a sheet of wafer paper. Dissolve and reduce the honey by putting it in a jar and standing this in boiling water for half-an-hour. When the sugar comes to the boil add the cream of tartar and boil the syrup to 265° Fahrenheit. Before this temperature is reached start whisking the whites of eggs in a copper bowl until they are fairly stiff. Then add the boiling sugar carefully to the eggs, stirring all the time. Place the bowl over the boiling water, still stirring carefully. After five minutes add the dissolved honey, the chopped almonds, nuts and cherries, and last of all a few drops of orange-flower water. Continue stirring the nougat for a few minutes, then drop a small piece of the mixture in cold water. If it is sufficiently cooked it can easily be formed with the fingers into a fairly firm ball. When quite cooked, pour the mixture on to the prepared slab between the bars, and cover the nougat with wafer paper. When it is sufficiently set, cut into pieces.

Rahati-l-holkum
Efendi Turabi, *A Manual of Turkish Cookery* (London, 1862)

Put in a very clean stewpan two pounds and three-quarters of loaf-sugar, with four quarts of water, and stir with a wooden spoon until the sugar is dissolved; then set it on a moderate charcoal fire, and immediately add eight ounces and a half of fine wheat starch by degrees, stirring it at the same time so as to prevent it getting lumpy, and continue stirring it from the bottom of the pan until it forms a smooth substance; then take a little out and let drop a few drops on powdered sugar. If it moistens or absorbs the sugar it is not done, and if it does not it is done. Then mix a little musk, the size of a small pea, in a little less than quarter of a pint of rose-water, and add this to it; stir it for half a minute longer, then take it off and put it in a convenient dish or a plated pan about half an inch deep which you have previously oiled with almond oil. When cold cut it in pieces an inch broad and two long, and dip them in sifted sugar mixed with half the quantity of fine wheat starch.

References

1 Sweet, Candy or Confection?

1 Tim Richardson, *Sweets: A History of Temptation* (London, 2002), pp. 53–4.
2 Henry Weatherley, *A Treatise on the Art of Boiling Sugar* (Philadelphia, PA, 1865), pp. 7–8.
3 Richardson, *Sweets*, p. 162.
4 Tsugita Sato, *Sugar in the Social Life of Medieval Islam* (Leiden, 2015), p. 164.
5 Michael Krondl, *Sweet Invention: A History of Dessert* (Chicago, IL, 2011), pp. 255–6.
6 Gaitri Pagrach-Chandra, *Sugar and Spice: Sweets and Treats from Around the World* (London, 2012), p. 77.
7 Priscilla Mary Işın, ed., *A King's Confectioner in the Orient: Friedrich Unger, Court Confectioner to King Otto I of Greece* (London, 2003), pp. 27–35.
8 Anil Kishore Sinha, *Anthropology of Sweetmeats* (New Delhi, 2000), pp. 75–6.
9 Richard Hosking, *A Dictionary of Japanese Food* (Rutland, VT, 1997), p. 168.
10 Christian Daniels, 'Biology and Biological Technology: Agro-industries: Sugar Technology', in Joseph Needham, Christian Daniels and Nicholas K. Menzies, *Science and Civilisation in China VI, Part III* (Cambridge, 1996), pp. 69–77.
11 Krondl, *Sweet Invention*, p. 6.

2 The Magic of Sugar

1 E. Skuse, *Skuse's Complete Confectioner,* 10th edn (London, *c.* 1900), p. 1.

2 See Harold McGee, *McGee on Food and Cooking* (London, 2004), p. 682 for fuller details.

3 Tsugita Sato, *Sugar in the Social Life of Medieval Islam* (Leiden, 2015), p. 47.

4 Simon I. Leon, *An Encyclopedia of Candy and Ice-cream Making* (New York, 1959), p. 368.

5 Tim Richardson, *Sweets: A History of Temptation* (London, 2002), pp. 106–7.

6 E. Skuse, *Confectioner's Handbook and Practical Guide*, 2nd edn (London, *c.* 1890), p. 50.

7 Andrew Dalby, *Dangerous Tastes: The Story of Spices* (London, 2000), p. 27.

8 Christian Daniels, 'Biology and Biological Technology: Agro-industries: Sugar Technology', in Joseph Needham, Christian Daniels and Nicholas K. Menzies, *Science and Civilisation in China VI, Part III* (Cambridge, 1996), p. 74.

9 Sir Hugh Plat, *Delightes for Ladies*, with an introduction by G. E. Fussell and Kathleen Rosemary Fussell (London, 1948), p. 38.

10 Skuse, *Confectioner's Handbook and Practical Guide*, 2nd edn, p. 50.

11 Henry Weatherley, *A Treatise on the Art of Boiling Sugar* (Philadelphia, PA, 1865), p. 42.

12 Keith Stavely and Kathleen Fitzgerald, 'Fudge', in *The Oxford Companion to Sugar and Sweets*, ed. Darra Goldstein (Oxford, 2015), p. 287.

13 Leon, *An Encyclopedia of Candy and Ice-cream Making*, p. 214.

14 Gaitri Pagrach-Chandra, *Sugar and Spice: Sweets and Treats from Around the World* (London, 2012), p. 107.

15 From the entry for 'praline', n., at www.oed.com.

16 Helen Nearing and Scott Nearing, *The Maple Sugar Book* (New York, 1970), pp. 22–7.

17 Weatherley, *A Treatise on the Art of Boiling Sugar*, p. 7.

18 Ibid., p. 6.

19 Skuse, *Skuse's Complete Confectioner*, p. 1.

20 Wendy A. Woloson, *Refined Tastes: Sugar, Confectionery and Consumers in Nineteenth-century America* (Baltimore, MD, 2002), p. 34.

21 McGee, *McGee on Food and Cooking*, p. 690.

22 Laura Mason, *Sugar Plums and Sherbet* (Totnes, 1998), p. 83.

23 Sato, *Sugar in the Social Life of Medieval Islam*, p. 164.

24 Knut Boeser, ed., *The Elixirs of Nostradamus* (London, 1995), pp. 150–53.

25 'How is Rock Candy Made?', www.attractionsblackpool. co.uk/Blackpool_Rock.htm, accessed 17 November 2016.

26 Henry Mayhew, *London Labour and the London Poor* (London, 1864), p. 216; Weatherley, *A Treatise on the Art of Boiling Sugar*, p. 32.

27 Priscilla Mary Işın, ed., *A King's Confectioner in the Orient: Friedrich Unger, Court Confectioner to King Otto I of Greece* (London, 2003), p. 99.

28 Mary Işın, *Sherbet and Spice* (London, 2013), pp. 137–8.

29 Christian Daniels, 'Biology and Biological Technology', p. 78.

30 Beth Kracklauer, 'Toffee', in *The Oxford Companion to Sugar and Sweets*, ed. Darra Goldstein (Oxford, 2015), pp. 727–8.

31 Weatherley, *A Treatise on the Art of Boiling Sugar*, pp. 7–8.

32 Skuse, *Confectioner's Handbook and Practical Guide*, p. 37.

33 Quoted by Richardson in *Sweets*, p. 35.

34 Skuse, *Skuse's Complete Confectioner*, p. 67.

35 Wikipedia hosts a worldwide 'list of chocolate bar brands', including details of fillings.

36 Pagrach-Chandra, *Sugar and Spice*, p. 43.

3 Spice and Everything Nice

1 Simon I. Leon, *An Encyclopedia of Candy and Ice-cream Making* (New York, 1959), p. 47.

2 Sally Butcher, *Persia in Peckham: Recipes from Persepolis* (Totnes, 2012), p. 304.

3 Christian Daniels, 'Biology and Biological Technology: Agro-industries: Sugar Technology', in Joseph Needham, Christian Daniels and Nicholas K. Menzies, *Science and Civilisation in China VI, Part III* (Cambridge, 1996), p. 78.

4 E. Skuse, *Skuse's Complete Confectioner,* 10th edn (London, *c.* 1900), p. 62.

5 Jane Levi, 'Nougat', in *The Oxford Companion to Sugar and Sweets*, ed. Darra Goldstein (Oxford, 2015), p. 486.

6 Mary Işın, *Sherbet and Spice* (London, 2013), pp. 127–8.

7 Ibid., p. 127.

8 Knut Boeser, ed., *The Elixirs of Nostradamus* (London, 1995), p. 149.

9 Tim Richardson, *Sweets: A History of Temptation* (London, 2002), p. 133.

10 Daniels, 'Biology and Biological Technology', p. 69.

11 E. Skuse, *Confectioner's Handbook and Practical Guide*, 2nd edn (London, *c.* 1890), p. 64.

12 Richard Hosking, *A Dictionary of Japanese Food* (Rutland, VT, 1997), p. 84.

13 Henry Weatherley, *A Treatise on the Art of Boiling Sugar* (Philadelphia, PA, 1865), p. 110.

14 Skuse, *Confectioner's Handbook and Practical Guide*, p. 64.

15 See www.tictacuk.com, accessed 13 November 2016.

16 Joël Glen Brenner, 'M&M's', in *The Oxford Companion to Sugar and Sweets*, p. 415.

17 Priscilla Mary Işın, ed., *A King's Confectioner in the Orient: Friedrich Unger, Court Confectioner to King Otto I of Greece* (London, 2003), p. 22.

18 Elizabeth David, *Italian Food* (London, 1987), p. 198.

19 J. Haldar, *Bengal Sweets* (Calcutta, 1948), pp. 162–3; Boeser, *The Elixirs of Nostradamus*, p. 91.

20 Daniels, 'Biology and Biological Technology', pp. 80–81.

21 Rachel Laudan, 'Dulche de Leche', in *The Oxford Companion to Sugar and Sweets*, p. 230.

22 Doreen Fernandez, *Tikim: Essays on Philippine Food and Culture* (Manila, 1994), p. 97.

23 Colleen Taylor-Sen, 'India', in *The Oxford Companion to Sugar and Sweets*, p. 357.

24 Yamuna Devi, *Lord Krishna's Cuisine: The Art of Indian Vegetarian Cooking* (London, 1990), p. 628.

25 Ibid., p. 592.

26 Haldar, *Bengal Sweets*, p. 73.

27 Colleen Taylor-Sen, 'The Portuguese Influence on Bengali Cuisine', in *Food on the Move: Proceedings of the Oxford Symposium on Food and Cookery*, ed. Harlan Walker (Totnes, 1996), p. 292.

28 Haldar, *Bengal Sweets*, p. 131.

29 Chitrita Banerji, *Life and Food in Bengal* (London, 1991), p. 132.

30 Su-Mei Yu, 'Thai Egg-based Sweets: The Legend of Thao Thong Keap-Ma', in *Gastronomica: The Journal of Food and Culture*, III/3 (2003), pp. 54–9.

31 Gaitri Pagrach-Chandra, *Sugar and Spice: Sweets and Treats from Around the World* (London, 2012), p. 67.

4 Some Oddities

1 Michael Krondl, *Sweet Invention: A History of Dessert* (Chicago, IL, 2011), p. 139.

2 Ivan Day, *Royal Sugar Sculpture: 600 Years of Splendour* (Bowes, 2002), p. 23.

3 Richard Hosking, *A Dictionary of Japanese Food* (Rutland, VT, 1997), pp. 234–5.

4 Mary Işın, *Sherbet and Spice* (London, 2013), p. 81.

5 Gaitri Pagrach-Chandra, *Sugar and Spice: Sweets and Treats from Around the World* (London, 2012), p. 8.

6 E. Skuse, *Skuse's Complete Confectioner,* 10th edn (London, *c.* 1900), p. 67.

7 Compton MacKenzie, *Echoes* (London, 1954), p. 60.

8 E. Skuse, *Confectioner's Handbook and Practical Guide*, 3rd edn (London, *c.* 1892), pp. 53–4.

9 Simon I. Leon, *An Encyclopedia of Candy and Ice-cream Making* (New York, 1959), p. 409.

10 See www.magiccandyfactory.com, accessed 9 May 2016.

11 Işin, *Sherbet and Spice*, p. 161.

12 Harley Spiller, 'Chewing Gum', in *The Oxford Companion to Sugar and Sweets*, ed. Darra Goldstein (Oxford, 2015), p. 128.

13 Ibid., p. 130.

14 Robert Hendrickson, *The Great American Chewing Gum Book* (Radnor, PA, 1976), pp. 83–4.

5 Manufacturers and Consumers

1 John Gerarde, *The Herball or Generall Historie of Plants* (London, 1597), p. 34.

2 May Whyte, *High-class Sweetmaking* (Birkenhead, *c.* 1910), p. vii.

3 Samira Kawash, *Candy: A Century of Panic and Pleasure* (New York, 2013), p. 135.

4 Robert Campbell, *The London Tradesman* (London, 1747), p. 278.

5 Leatherhead Food Research Association, *The Confectionery Market: A Global Analysis* (London, 2002), p. 8.

6 Carla Zanetos Scully, 'The 2013 Top 100 Candy Companies in the World', www.candyindustry.com, 11 February 2013.

7 Ralph Rylance, *The Epicure's Almanack; or, Guide to Good Living* (London, 1815), p. 103.

8 Anon., *A Closet for Ladies and Gentlewomen* (London, 1608), p. 39.

9 Wendy A. Woloson, *Refined Tastes: Sugar, Confectionery and Consumers in Nineteenth-century America* (Baltimore, MD, 2002), p. 44.

10 Kawash, *Candy*, p. 38.

11 Nicholas Whittaker, *Sweet Talk: The Secret History of Confectionery* (London, 1998), pp. 10–11.

12 Toni Risson, 'A Pocket of Change in Post-war Australia: Confectionery and the End of Childhood', in *Pockets of Change: Adaption and Cultural Transition*, ed. Tricia Hopton, Adam Atkinson, Jane Stadler and Peta Mitchell (Lanham, MD, 2011), p. 114.

13 Anil Kishore Sinha, *Anthropology of Sweetmeats* (New Delhi, 2000), p. 193.

14 Leatherhead Food Research Association, *The Confectionery Market*, p. 10.

15 Ibid., p. 15.

16 Alice G. Walton, 'How Much Sugar are Americans Eating?', *Forbes Magazine,* www.forbes.com, 30 August 2012.

17 John Burnett, *Plenty and Want* (London, 1983), p. 341.

18 Quoted in C. Anne Wilson, *Food and Drink in Britain* (London, 1991), p. 300.

19 Robert Lustig, *Fat Chance: The Hidden Truth About Sugar, Obesity and Disease* (London, 2013), p. 118.

20 WHO Guideline, *Sugars Intake for Adults and Children* (Geneva, 2015), p. 4.

6 Sweets and Festivity

1 Jennifer Stead, 'Bowers of Bliss', in *Banquetting Stuffe: The Fare and Social Background of the Tudor and Stuart Banquet*, ed. C. Anne Wilson (Edinburgh, 1991), pp. 146–7.

2 François Massialot, *The Court and Country Cook* (London, 1702), p. 125.

3 Samira Kawash, *Candy: A Century of Panic and Pleasure* (New York, 2013), p. 269.

4 F. P. Wilson, ed., *The Batchelars Banquet* (Oxford, 1929), p. 21.

5 William Gunter, *Gunter's Confectioner's Oracle* (London, 1830), pp. 60–61.

6 Sir Hugh Plat, *Delightes for Ladies*, with an introduction by G. E. Fussell and Kathleen Rosemary Fussell (London, 1948), p. 28.

7 Ivan Day, 'Bridecup and Cake: The Ceremonial Food and Drink of the Wedding Procession', in *Food and the Rites of Passage*, ed. Laura Mason (Totnes, 2002).

8 Gaitri Pagrach-Chandra, *Sugar and Spice: Sweets and Treats from Around the World* (London, 2012), p. 113.

9 Ivan Day, *Royal Sugar Sculpture: 600 Years of Splendour* (Bowes, 2002).

10 Nancy Fasholt, *Clear Toy Candy* (Mechanicsburg, PA, 2010), p. 13.

11 Pagrach-Chandra, *Sugar and Spice*, p. 60.

12 C. F. Leyel and Olga Hartley, *The Gentle Art of Cookery* (London, 1929), p. 331.

13 Helen Saberi, *Noshe Djan: Afghan Food and Cookery* (London, 2000), p. 243.

14 George Borrow, *The Zincali, or An Account of the Gypsies of Spain* (London, 1893) pp. 190–91.

15 Su-Mei Yu, 'Thai Egg-based Sweets: The Legend of Thao Thong Keap-Ma', in *Gastronomica: The Journal of Food and Culture*, III/3 (2003), pp. 54–9.

16 Michael Krondl, *Sweet Invention: A History of Dessert* (Chicago, IL, 2011), p. 16.

17 Anil Kishore Sinha, *Anthropology of Sweetmeats* (New Delhi, 2000), p. 100.

18 Madhur Jaffrey, *Madhur Jaffrey's Indian Cookery* (London, 1982), p. 7.

19 Christian Daniels, 'Biology and Biological Technology: Agro-industries: Sugar Technology', in Joseph Needham, Christian Daniels and Nicholas K. Menzies, *Science and Civilisation in China VI, Part III* (Cambridge, 1996), p. 72.

20 Carol Stepanchuk and Charles Wong, *Mooncakes and Hungry Ghosts* (San Francisco, CA, 1991), p. 7.

Select Bibliography

Anon., *A Closet for Ladies and Gentlewomen* (London, 1608)

Apell, Charles, *Twentieth Century Candy Teacher* (USA: place not given, 1912)

Banerji, Chitrita, *Life and Food in Bengal* (London, 1991)

Boeser, Knut, ed., *The Elixirs of Nostradamus* (London, 1995)

Burnett, John, *Plenty and Want* (London, 1983)

Butcher, Sally, *Persia in Peckham: Recipes from Persepolis* (Totnes, 2012)

Carmichael, Elizabeth, and Chloe Sayer, *The Skeleton at the Feast: The Day of the Dead in Mexico* (London, 1991)

Dalby, Andrew, *Dangerous Tastes: The Story of Spices* (London, 2000)

Daniels, Christian, 'Biology and Biological Technology: Agro-industries: Sugar Technology', in Joseph Needham, Christian Daniels and Nicholas K. Menzies, *Science and Civilisation in China VI, Part III* (Cambridge, 1996)

Day, Ivan, *Royal Sugar Sculpture: 600 Years of Splendour* (Bowes, 2002)

Deerr, Noël, *The History of Sugar* (London, 1949)

Devi, Yamuna, *Lord Krishna's Cuisine: The Art of Indian Vegetarian Cooking* (London, 1990)

Eales, Mary, *Mrs Mary Eale's Receipts [1718] reproduced from the edition of 1733* (London, 1985)

Fasholt, Nancy, *Clear Toy Candy* (Mechanicsburg, PA, 2010)

Fernandez, Doreen G., and Edilberto N. Alegre, *Sarap: Essays on Philippine Food* (Manila, 1988)

Fernandez, Doreen, *Tikim: Essays on Philippine Food and Culture* (Manila, 1994)

Gilliers, Joseph, *Le Cannameliste français* (Nancy, 1751)

Goldstein, Darra, ed., *The Oxford Companion to Sugar and Sweets* (Oxford, 2015)

Gunter, William, *Gunter's Confectioner's Oracle* (London, 1830)

Haldar, J., *Bengal Sweets* (Calcutta, 1948)

Hendrickson, Robert, *The Great American Chewing Gum Book* (Radnor, PA, 1976)

Henisch, Bridget Ann, *Cakes and Characters* (London, 1984)

Hess, Karen, *Martha Washington's Booke of Cookery* (New York, 1981)

Hosking, Richard, *A Dictionary of Japanese Food* (Rutland, VT, 1997)

Işın, Mary, *Sherbet and Spice* (London, 2013)

Işın, Priscilla Mary, ed., *A King's Confectioner in the Orient: Friedrich Unger, Court Confectioner to King Otto I of Greece* (London, 2003)

Jarrin, William Alexis, *The Italian Confectioner* (London, 1820)

Kawash, Samira, *Candy: A Century of Panic and Pleasure* (New York, 2013)

Krondl, Michael, *Sweet Invention: A History of Dessert* (Chicago, IL, 2011)

Lees, R., and E. B. Jackson, *Sugar and Chocolate Confectionery Manufacture* (Aylesbury, 1973)

Leon, Simon I., *An Encyclopedia of Candy and Ice-cream Making* (New York, 1959)

Lustig, Robert, *Fat Chance: The Hidden Truth About Sugar, Obesity and Disease* (London, 2013)

McGee, Harold, *McGee on Food and Cooking* (London, 2004)

Mrs McLintock, *Mrs McLintock's Receipts for Cookery and Pastry-work 1736*, reproduced from the original with an introduction and glossary by Iseabail Macleod (Aberdeen, 1986)

McNiell, F. Marian, *The Scots Kitchen: Its Lore and Recipes* (London, 1963)

Mason, Laura, *Sugar Plums and Sherbet* (Totnes, 1998)

Mintz, Sidney W., *Sweetness and Power: The Place of Sugar in Modern History* (New York, 1985)

Nearing, Helen, and Scott Nearing, *The Maple Sugar Book* (New York, 1970)

Oddy, Derek J., *From Plain Fare to Fusion Food: British Diet from the 1890s to the 1990s* (London, 2003)

Opie, Robert, *Sweet Memories* (London, 1988)

Pagrach-Chandra, Gaitri, *Sugar and Spice: Sweets and Treats from Around the World* (London, 2012)

Perrier-Robert, Annie, *Les Friandises et leurs secrets* (Paris, 1986)

The Picayune, *The Picayune's Creole Cookbook*, 2nd edn (New York, 1971)

Piemontese, Alessio, *The Secretes of the Reverend Maister Alexis of Piemont*, trans. William Warde (London, 1562)

Plat, Sir Hugh, *Delightes for Ladies,* with an introduction by G. E. Fussell and Kathleen Rosemary Fussell (London, 1948)

Raffald, Elizabeth, *The Experienced English Housekeeper [1769], with an introduction by Roy Shipperbottom* (London, 1996)

Richardson, Tim, *Sweets: A History of Temptation* (London, 2002)

Rigg, Annie, *Sweet Things: Chocolates, Candies, Caramels and Marshmallows – To Make and Give* (London, 2013)

Risson, Toni, 'A Pocket of Change in Post-war Australia: Confectionery and the End of Childhood', in *Pockets of Change: Adaption and Cultural Transition*, ed. Tricia Hopton, Adam Atkinson, Jane Stadler and Peta Mitchell (Lanham, MD, 2011)

Saberi, Helen, *Noshe Djan: Afghan Food and Cookery* (London, 2000)

Sato, Tsugita, *Sugar in the Social Life of Medieval Islam* (Leiden, 2015)

Sinha, Anil Kishore, *Anthropology of Sweetmeats* (New Delhi, 2000)

Skuse, E., *Confectioner's Handbook and Practical Guide*, 2nd edn (London, *c.* 1890)

—, *Confectioner's Handbook and Practical Guide*, 3rd edn (London, *c.* 1892)

—, *Skuse's Complete Confectioner,* 10th edn (London, *c.* 1900)

Smith, Andrew F., *Sugar: A Global History* (London, 2015)

Weatherley, Henry, *A Treatise on the Art of Boiling Sugar* (Philadelphia, PA, 1865)

Whittaker, Nicholas, *Sweet Talk: The Secret History of Confectionery* (London, 1998)

Whyte, May, *High-class Sweetmaking* (Birkenhead, *c.* 1910)

Wilson, C. Anne, *The Book of Marmalade* (London, 1985)

—, ed., *Banquetting Stuffe: The Fare and Social Background of the Tudor and Stuart Banquet* (Edinburgh, 1991)

Woloson, Wendy A., *Refined Tastes: Sugar, Confectionery and Consumers in Nineteenth-century America* (Baltimore, MD, 2002)

Yudkin, John, *Pure, White and Deadly* (London, 1986)

Websites and Associations

A useful website for exploring some of the complexities
of Indian confections:
www.ambalafoods.com

About liquorice brands, everywhere:
www.licorice.org/index.htm

A good history of liquorice:
www.madeinsouthitalytoday.com/history-of-licorice.php

All large confectionery companies have websites, which
include their histories. Mondēlez International now owns
many well-known brands and their website includes
a corporate timeline:
www.mondelezinternational.com

The Nestlé website, likewise, includes a useful timeline:
www.nestle.co.uk

CAOBISCO is a useful source of statistics and information
on the industry in the EU:
www.caobisco.eu

The USA equivalent is The National Confectioner's Association:
www.candyusa.com

The Professional Manufacturing Confectioner's Association also maintain a useful website:
http://pmca.com

Places to Visit

In the USA, Schimpff's Confectionery have a candy museum and offer demonstrations:
www.schimpffs.com

Hershey's offer the opportunity to create one's own chocolate bar at their visitor centres:
www.hersheys.com/chocolateworld

In the UK The North of England Open Air Folk Museum includes a confectioner's shop from the late nineteenth century, with demonstrations:
www.beamish.org.uk

The manufacture of seaside rock and other confectionery can be viewed at John Bull Confectioners:
www.john-bull.com

In Berlin, The Sugar Museum includes material on the uses and display of sugar:
www.sdtb.de/Zucker-Museum

The Demel Konditorei was founded in 1786 and continues to operate in traditional style in Vienna:
http://demel.at

Nicolas Stohrer founded a pâtisserie in Paris in 1730 which still operates from the original premises:
www.stohrer.fr

Also in Paris, À la Mère de Famille is a confectionery shop
whose origins lie in the early eighteenth century:
www.lameredefamille.com

In Turkey, Şekerci Cafer Erol provides a wide range of Turkish
sweets displayed in traditional fashion:
www.sekercicafererol.com

Traditional milk-based Bengali sweets can be purchased
in Kolkata:
www.kcdas.co.in

Acknowledgements

This book is the product of many years of research, observation and discussion. Over that time, numerous individuals and organizations have provided expertise and practical help, with many thanks to:

Jane Baker; Sultan Barakat; Jeremy Cherfas; Ivan Day; Ruth Grant; Sasha Grigorieva; Vicky Hayward; Mehdi Hojat; Richard Hosking; Alex Hutchinson at Nestlé Archives, York; Mary Işın; Charlotte Knox; Fabrizia Lanza; Janalice Merry; Nuray Ösaslan; Gaitri Pagrach-Chandra; Professor Ugo Palma; Glynna Prentice; Gillian Riley; Joe and Emma Roberts; Helen Saberi; Mary Taylor Simeti; Agnes Winter; the staff of the Borthwick Institute, University of York; the staff of Dobsons of Elland; Mr G. K. Noon at Royal Halva; and two people both now sadly deceased, who were of enormous help when I first started collecting material on the subject many years ago, Alan Davidson and Doreen Fernandez. Last but not least, thanks to all at Reaktion Books, especially Michael Leaman, Andy Smith, Becca Wright, Martha Jay and Harry Gilonis.

Photo Acknowledgements

The author and publishers wish to express their thanks to the below sources of illustrative material and/or permission to reproduce it. Some locations of artworks are also given below, in the interests of brevity.

Alte Pinakothek, Munich: p. 127; photo Amoret Tanner Collection/ Rex Features/Shutterstock: p. 20; collection of the author: pp. 10, 43; photos by the author: pp. 9, 16, 31, 38–9, 41, 49, 53, 60, 64, 67, 72, 82, 83, 86, 87, 96, 111, 125, 130; photo courtesy of the author: p. 93; photo baument/BigStockPhoto: p. 45; photo © Bibliothèque Forney/Roger-Viollet/Rex Features/Shutterstock: p. 13; photo © Jacques Boyer/Roger-Viollet/Rex Features/Shutterstock: p. 71; Casa Museu Anselmo Braamcamp Freire, Santarém: p. 107; Cleveland Museum of Art: p. 134; from Denis Diderot and Jean le Rond d'Alembert, *L'Encyclopédie . . . recueil de planches, sur les sciences . . .*, vol. xx (Paris, 1768): p. 68; photo fotograv/iStock International: pp. 76–7; photo John Gay/Historic England/Mary Evans Picture Library: p. 27; from Joseph Gilliers, *Le Cannameliste français, ou Nouvelle instruction pour ceux qui desirent d'apprendre l'office, rédigé en forme de dictionnaire* (Nancy, 1751): p. 93; photo huyendesigner/ BigStockPhoto: p. 79; photos Mary Işın: pp. 63, 104; photo Fabrizia Lanza: p. 126; photos Library of Congress, Washington, DC (Prints and Photographs Division): pp. 33, 113 (British Cartoon Prints Collection), 121, 132; location unknown (sold via Sotheby's in 2010): p. 47; from Johannes and Caspaares Luiken, *Het menselijk*

image in the manner specified by the author or licensor (but not in any way that suggests that these parties endorse them or their use of the work).

Index

italic numbers refer to illustrations; **bold** to recipes